The Israeli Air For
Part One - 1948 to 19...

CONTENTS

Chapter 1:   Page 3

Birth and the War of Independence

Chapter 2:   Page 26

Trials of a fledgling Air Force -
developing an air force

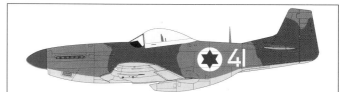

Chapter 3:   Page 42

The Sinai Campaign
'Operation Kadesh' and Suez

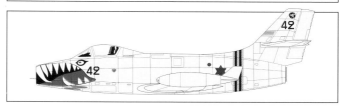

Chapter 4:   Page 54

The Decade of Calm
New thinking - New equipment

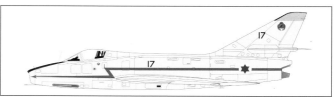

Chapter 5:   Page 70

The Six Day War
The Path to War

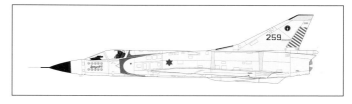

Chapter 6:   Page 88

Israeli Air Force Colours
and Markings 1948 - 1967

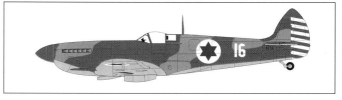

Inside covers: examples of IAF Squadron badges used between 1948 and 1967.

Scale Aircraft Monographs
Camouflage and Markings
'The Israeli Air Force
Part One: 1948 to 1969'
by Ray Ball

Artwork by
David Howley
Peter Scott
Jon Freeman

Cover Artwork by
Mark Rolfe

Series Editor: Neil Robinson

Design and layout: Steve Page

Published by: Guideline Publications
Tel: 01582 505999

Printed by Regal Litho Ltd.
352 Selbourne Road
Luton, Bedfordshire LU4 8NU

Fouga Magister of the Flying School, Hatzerim, circa 1967

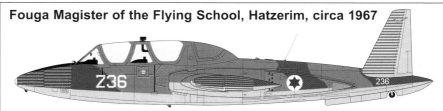

The standard Israeli Air Force camouflage scheme (from the mid-1950s to the mid/late 1960s) was in an Israeli manufactured paint, Dark Blue and Medium Brown uppersurfaces with Light Grey undersides, with the national insignia *Magen David* in six positions. The Fouga Magisters of the Flying School had Day-Glo stripes applied to the nose, tip tanks and fins, with white identification numerals on the fuselage.

OTHER TITLES AVAILABLE IN THIS SERIES:
No. 1 RAF FIGHTERS 1945-1950 UK BASED
No. 2 THE BATTLE FOR BRITAIN - RAF: MAY TO DECEMBER 1940

The Israeli Air Force Part One 1948 to 1969

Six tiny dots appeared over the sea and as they came closer, the citizens of Tel Aviv knew the Egyptians had returned. The air-raid sirens wailed as they had many times these last few weeks. Egyptian Air Force Douglas C-47 Dakotas, converted into bombers and escorted by Spitfires, had carried out several raids before, one hitting the Central Bus Station and causing many casualties. But today was 3 June 1948, and the citizens were about to become aware of the Israeli Air Force.

As the aircraft neared the City the escorting Spitfires were seen to break away from the Dakotas as another dot appeared out of the sun and closed on the formation. The new dot was seen to chase a Dakota and, after short burst from its guns, send it crashing into the shoreline. The second Dakota was caught directly over the City sea front, giving the citizens a grandstand view and again, after a brief burst of fire, was seen to dive out of control towards Arab held land. By this time, the *Magen David* (Shield of David) was visible on the wings of this mysterious fighter aircraft and the citizens of Tel Aviv were now aware that Israel had an Air Force, and that Air Force had made its presence felt.

Fifty years later and the whole world is aware that Israel has an Air Force because it has made its presence felt on many occasions. Its exploits in the defence of the State have become legendary and Israel holds its Air Force members in high regard. It has earned International respect for its achievements and professionalism both in times of conflict and for its humanitarian and relief work carried out in many parts of the world. This is the story of that Air Force from its humble beginnings in 1948 to the high-tech age of today.

Acknowledgements

You learn a lot about yourself when you write a book - or two! Not least how gullible you are!! Having written 'Part Three' of the IAF article for the March 2000 issue of *Scale Aircraft Modelling*, Neil asked me to write these books - and I forgot about the work involved!

In some ways, I welcomed the opportunity. There has been a lot of 'rubbish' printed about the Israeli Air Force so this was a chance to put some things right - *I certainly didn't want to add to the rubbish!* I decided to tell the story as it happened and, because these books are primarily aimed at model makers, attempted to give as much aircraft detail information as I could, if for no other reason than to further interest in the hobby, and the IAF.

My research has led me to challenge some beliefs I have held to be true, as new information came to light. More emerges all the time to improve our knowledge and adding to our fascination. This enrichment of our hobby comes from dedicated Israelis who have undertaken their own research and discovery. Former members of the IAF have also written books and articles about their experiences, adding to the pool of information. There are still gaps in our knowledge, particularly about the early years. Early aircraft were painted in green and brown camouflage schemes, in random patterns which can only be determined from photographs. Also the paint came from whatever sources were available at the time, and mixed accordingly, so the *exact* shades of brown and green might be unknown, although it is now known is that a major source of the paint was stocks of RAF Dark Green and Dark Earth left behind at former RAF airfields. There is therefore a degree of admitted speculation in some of the artwork but, hopefully, only regarding the *exact shade* of the colours involved.

My references have been exclusively Israeli, and I have strived to produce something that is informative and accurate, avoiding myth and speculation. Unlike other writers on the IAF, my avoidance of speculative information has also extended to Squadron Numbers. Except for the early period where the numbers were definitely known, I have referred to Squadrons by the names commonly used by the Israelis. The IAF still regard Squadron Numbers as sensitive and confidential and I am reliably informed that *not one* list of published numbers around today is correct. Only the IAF know the true position, so I will respect their views and wait until *they* reveal the true information.

Another thing you learn is that you cannot produce a book by yourself. Invariably you need further information and to check your references, and in this case, I also needed to check my translations. I freely and gratefully acknowledge the help and guidance I received from Raanan Weiss of *IsraDecals*, who has been a true friend for many years. He has been my mentor on this project, as well as filling several gaps in my knowledge and assisting with providing photographs, in spite of other demands on his time. He has my eternal gratitude for all he has done. Others I must thank include Yoav Efrati who also supplied invaluable advice and photographs, and Guri and Asher Roth for their patience as I checked out references and translations. Asher is another long term friend and President of IPMS Israel. My many other sources of reference material were also all Israeli, but it would fill a book to mention them all individually by name, so I take this opportunity to collectively thank them all - for sharing their experiences in numerous telephone calls, letters, e-mails, books, articles and other publications.

Lastly, as I locked myself away and started babbling in a foreign language, my family did detect a change in my behaviour! My parents had seen this all before with my Law studies years ago, and only have themselves to blame for introducing me into the hobby in the first place. This hobby has given me friendships and pleasure so if I have not thanked them before, I do now. For my wife though this was a new experience. Although Neil Robinson was generous with his time (and always gave me 'yesterday' as the deadline), my time had other demands upon it and these began to conflict. It is not that we were not speaking to each other, it's just that we were speaking in different languages. Still coffee and understanding are universal, and I owe my wife 'big-time'. So I end these acknowledgements with a big 'thank you' to Janet and my son Christopher.

Ray Ball
Derbyshire
October 2000

About the author

I developed an interest in aircraft and model-making as a lad in the 1950s. At that time it was possible to go to the local branch of Woolworths and buy the latest release from Airfix for just 1/11d (9p), the most expensive was the Sunderland at 10/6d (52p). I have retained my interest ever since, although it has waned from time to time for College, Family and Work needs. My interest in the Israeli Air Force started in the 1960s, when information about their exploits began to be published in the magazines of the time. The news of the war in 1967 gripped my attention and I was astonished by their achiements in a war that was over in just six days. Since then I have collected information and reference material on the Israeli air Force and built a model collection that includes nearly every aircraft flown by the IAF.

I have made many Israeli friends and have been fortunate to visit many IAF airbases and see their aircraft first hand. (They are all *wrong* - not a bit like my models!). I am a member of IPMS(UK) and a former Hon Treasurer, and was leader of the IAF Special Interest Group from 1989 to 1996. My interest in the IAF today is as strong as it always has been. Their rescue and humanitarian work never hits the news as much as their other exploits, but I know, like me, they share a wish for peace in a Region that has been troubled by conflict for too long.
Ray Ball

Chapter 1

Birth and the War of Independence

Birth and Baptism

When 27 year old, former RAF Flight Lieutenant Modi Alon, flying an Avia S-199, shot down the two Dakotas, the State of Israel was less than three weeks old and the Air Force was still in the process of being formed - in reality, existing only as a title. However, the roots for an air force had been established many years before.

Jewish communities and settlements were scattered the length and breadth of Palestine, and the leaders knew that in times of conflict many of these settlements would be blockaded by their Arab neighbours. Supply and Communication to these cut-off sites could only be air. Each settlement had its *Haganah* (Defence Force) members, but these were largely ill-equipped ground forces with little formal training. As tensions increased between the Arab and Jewish communities, that was to change as the *Haganah* High Command improved training and established a strike arm, the *Palmach*. Linked to this was support for an air arm.

As early as the 1930s, the *Haganah* supported the formation of Gliding Clubs and encouraged its members to join. Permission was granted by the British Mandate Authority for the formation of Flying Clubs. The Carmel Club formed in 1932 at Carmel near Haifa, and the 'Flying Camel' Club formed soon afterwards. In the mid-1930s all the Flying Clubs were amalgamated into the 'Aero Club of Israel'.

The International Airport at Lydda (Lod) was opened in 1936 and a third flying club, 'Palestine Flying Services', was formed there the following year with a single Gipsy Moth G-ABMX. In addition

to training pilots, these clubs also trained the necessary ground crews with the essential engineering and other skills to support an aviation service. Palestine airspace began to be criss-crossed with light aircraft. A DH 82A Tiger Moth, registered VQ-PAN was brought to Palestine in 1938. From Poland, two RWD-8s were acquired, registered as VQ-PAG and VQ-PAK. The year 1938 also saw the arrival of Taylorcraft, Model A, VQ-PAH, followed by two Model BLs, VQ-PAI and VQ-PAJ the following year to the 'Palestine Flying Services'

Two aviation companies were also formed about this time, The Aviron (aircraft) Company in 1936, and Palestine Airways Ltd in 1937. Palestine Airways, a subsidiary, of Imperial Airways was a true commercial undertaking operating two Short Scions, VQ-PAA and VQ-PAB, a Short Scion Senior, VQ-PAD and a DH89 Rapide, VQ-PAC. As the Jewish population were reluctant to travel through Arab territory to Lydda Airport, Palestine Airways constructed a new airfield north of Tel Aviv near the Reading power Station, which served as Tel Aviv Airfield and as a base for the station operators, for the aircraft they used on communication work and power line inspections. Palestine Airways ceased to exist in 1940 when the RAF commandeered their aircraft for transport duties in the Western Desert.

Aviron had close links with the *Haganah*, becoming its civilian cover and as a source to acquire aircraft as well as operating them and training both pilots and ground crews. To start with, it acquired an RWD 8 and a Tiger Moth from the Aero Club, then in July 1939, two RWD-13s arrived registered as VQ-PAL

and VQ-PAM, followed by an RWD-15, VQ-PAE in December 1939. By this time Palestine Flying Services had folded and Aviron also acquired their business and three Taylorcrafts, giving them a presence at Lydda in addition to their base at Afikim in the Jordan Valley.

In 1939, The Palestine Commercial Aviation Co Ltd operated from Lydda with a single Fokker F-XVIII, VQ-PAF. Work on these civil aircraft and those of International Airlines flying to Palestine also served to increase the skills of the ground crews.

The outbreak of World War Two severely curtailed these flying operations in Israel, but many Jews in Palestine volunteered for the Allied cause serving in large numbers as both air and ground crews. At the time of Independence in 1948 the Jewish Community in Palestine contained over 2500 men and women who had served with the Allied Air Forces.

Partition

On 29 November 1947, the United Nations approved the partition of Palestine into separate Jewish and Arab States. The British Mandate was to end in May 1948. These events increased tension and conflict between the two sides. Fighting erupted, throughout Palestine, with Jewish settlements becoming isolated as predicted. By this time only the Aero Club of Israel and Aviron remained, and their aircraft began

Above: Two pilots of 101 Squadron pose in front of Avia S-199, D-115, at Herzliya, in the summer of 1948. D-115 participated in many missions before being destroyed in a landing accident when returning from an operation on 8 September 1948. The pilot, former RAF officer, Alex 'Sandy' Jacobs, survived the crash.

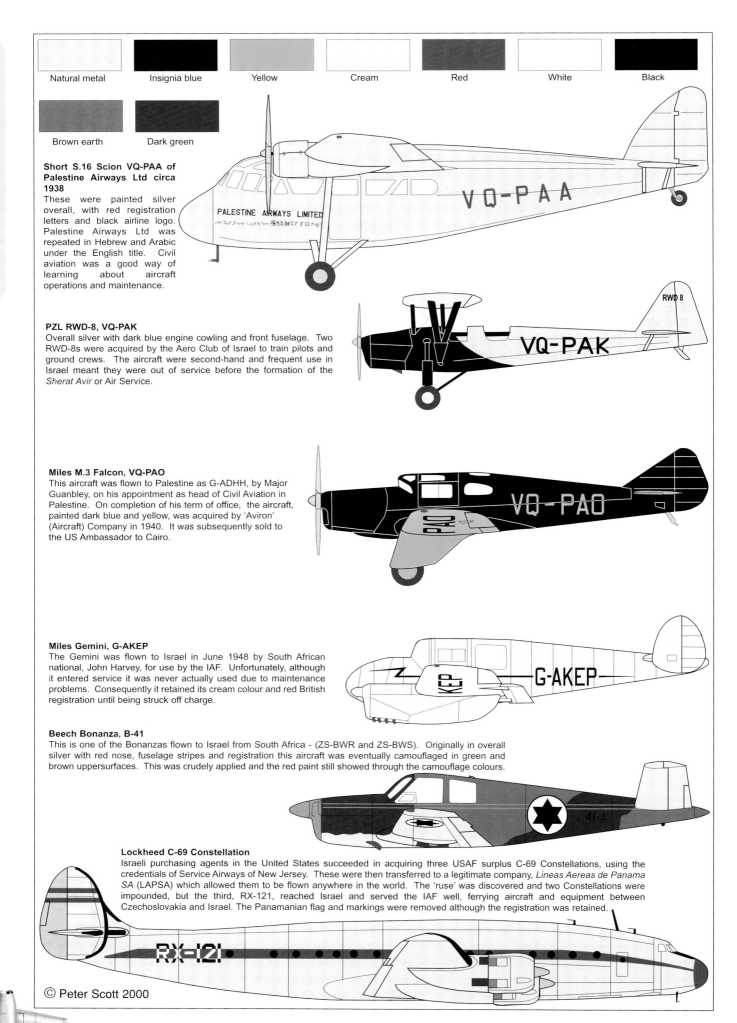

Natural metal | Insignia blue | Yellow | Cream | Red | White | Black

Brown earth | Dark green

Short S.16 Scion VQ-PAA of Palestine Airways Ltd circa 1938
These were painted silver overall, with red registration letters and black airline logo. Palestine Airways Ltd was repeated in Hebrew and Arabic under the English title. Civil aviation was a good way of learning about aircraft operations and maintenance.

PZL RWD-8, VQ-PAK
Overall silver with dark blue engine cowling and front fuselage. Two RWD-8s were acquired by the Aero Club of Israel to train pilots and ground crews. The aircraft were second-hand and frequent use in Israel meant they were out of service before the formation of the *Sherat Avir* or Air Service.

Miles M.3 Falcon, VQ-PAO
This aircraft was flown to Palestine as G-ADHH, by Major Guanbley, on his appointment as head of Civil Aviation in Palestine. On completion of his term of office, the aircraft, painted dark blue and yellow, was acquired by 'Aviron' (Aircraft) Company in 1940. It was subsequently sold to the US Ambassador to Cairo.

Miles Gemini, G-AKEP
The Gemini was flown to Israel in June 1948 by South African national, John Harvey, for use by the IAF. Unfortunately, although it entered service it was never actually used due to maintenance problems. Consequently it retained its cream colour and red British registration until being struck off charge.

Beech Bonanza, B-41
This is one of the Bonanzas flown to Israel from South Africa - (ZS-BWR and ZS-BWS). Originally in overall silver with red nose, fuselage stripes and registration this aircraft was eventually camouflaged in green and brown uppersurfaces. This was crudely applied and the red paint still showed through the camouflage colours.

Lockheed C-69 Constellation
Israeli purchasing agents in the United States succeeded in acquiring three USAF surplus C-69 Constellations, using the credentials of Service Airways of New Jersey. These were then transferred to a legitimate company, *Lineas Aereas de Panama SA* (LAPSA) which allowed them to be flown anywhere in the world. The 'ruse' was discovered and two Constellations were impounded, but the third, RX-121, reached Israel and served the IAF well, ferrying aircraft and equipment between Czechoslovakia and Israel. The Panamanian flag and markings were removed although the registration was retained.

© Peter Scott 2000

4

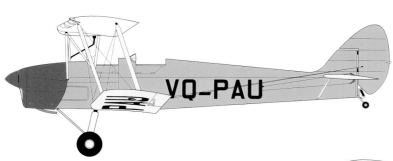

Tiger Moth, VQ-PAU
Overall yellow with red engine cowling and spinner. Acquired by the Aero Club in 1947, VQ-PAU was originally a DH-82C from Canada with an enclosed cockpit which was removed for *Sherut Avir* (Air Service) operations.

Taylorcraft, formerly VQ-PAI
The early aircraft of Aviran and *Sherut Avir* were cream yellow or silver dope with few exceptions. On commencement of hostilities, these aircraft were quickly camouflaged in brown and green uppersurfaces and given an IAF number in this case 'A-31'. The undersides were painted either grey, light blue or left in silver, depending what paint was available or not.

PZL RWD-13, VQ-PAM
This aircraft was operated by Aviron and *Sherut Avir* before going into IAF service as 'A-33'. These useful Polish light aircraft flew liaison and transport flights to outlying settlements all over Israel. Originally in overall silver, they too received green and brown camouflage in May 1948.

Auster Autocrat, VQ-PAS
Acquired by Aviran in 1946, the Aurocrat J/1 was a civilian version of the Army AOP.5. Painted silver with a red fuselage stripe, VQ-PAS went on to serve the Air Force on liaison duties as 'A-32' in brown and green camouflage.

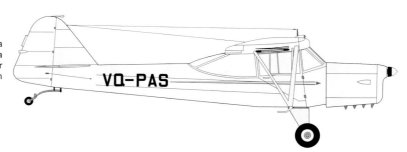

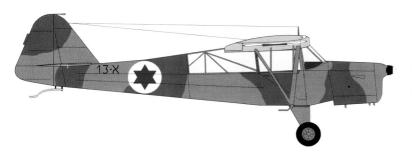

Auster AOP.3, A-13
One of twenty Austers purchased from surplus RAF stocks by Aviron in 1947. There were two AOP.3s in this batch, and these were extensively used by the IAF in the early days for liaison and supply work.

Auster AOP.5, A-11,
Another one of the twenty Austers acquired in 1947. This aircraft was painted the same as Taylorcraft VQ-PAI and given the same registration to disguise its origin. It was known as VQ-PAI/11. After Independence Day and the raid by the Egyptian Air Force on Sde Dov Airfield, it was camouflaged in green and brown and given the serial number A-11.

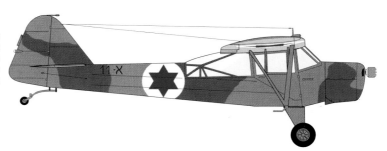

© M.D.Howley 2000

PART 1　CHAPTER 1

5

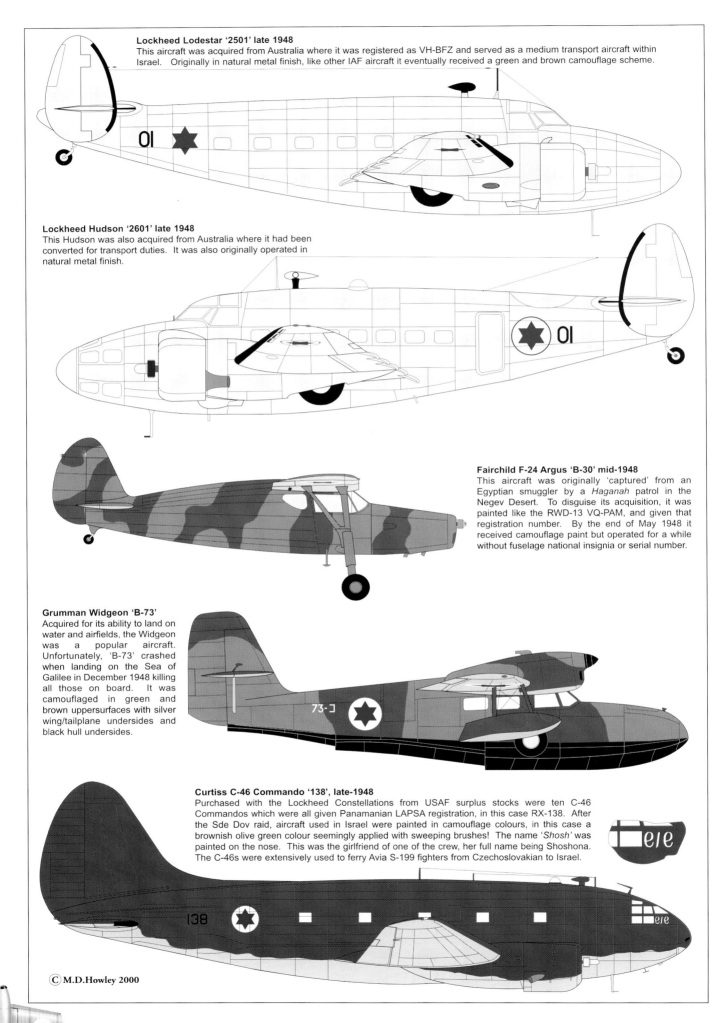

ISRAELI AIR FORCE 1948-1967

Lockheed Lodestar '2501' late 1948
This aircraft was acquired from Australia where it was registered as VH-BFZ and served as a medium transport aircraft within Israel. Originally in natural metal finish, like other IAF aircraft it eventually received a green and brown camouflage scheme.

Lockheed Hudson '2601' late 1948
This Hudson was also acquired from Australia where it had been converted for transport duties. It was also originally operated in natural metal finish.

Fairchild F-24 Argus 'B-30' mid-1948
This aircraft was originally 'captured' from an Egyptian smuggler by a *Haganah* patrol in the Negev Desert. To disguise its acquisition, it was painted like the RWD-13 VQ-PAM, and given that registration number. By the end of May 1948 it received camouflage paint but operated for a while without fuselage national insignia or serial number.

Grumman Widgeon 'B-73'
Acquired for its ability to land on water and airfields, the Widgeon was a popular aircraft. Unfortunately, 'B-73' crashed when landing on the Sea of Galilee in December 1948 killing all those on board. It was camouflaged in green and brown uppersurfaces with silver wing/tailplane undersides and black hull undersides.

Curtiss C-46 Commando '138', late-1948
Purchased with the Lockheed Constellations from USAF surplus stocks were ten C-46 Commandos which were all given Panamanian LAPSA registration, in this case RX-138. After the Sde Dov raid, aircraft used in Israel were painted in camouflage colours, in this case a brownish olive green colour seemingly applied with sweeping brushes! The name '*Shosh*' was painted on the nose. This was the girlfriend of one of the crew, her full name being Shoshona. The C-46s were extensively used to ferry Avia S-199 fighters from Czechoslovakian to Israel.

© M.D.Howley 2000

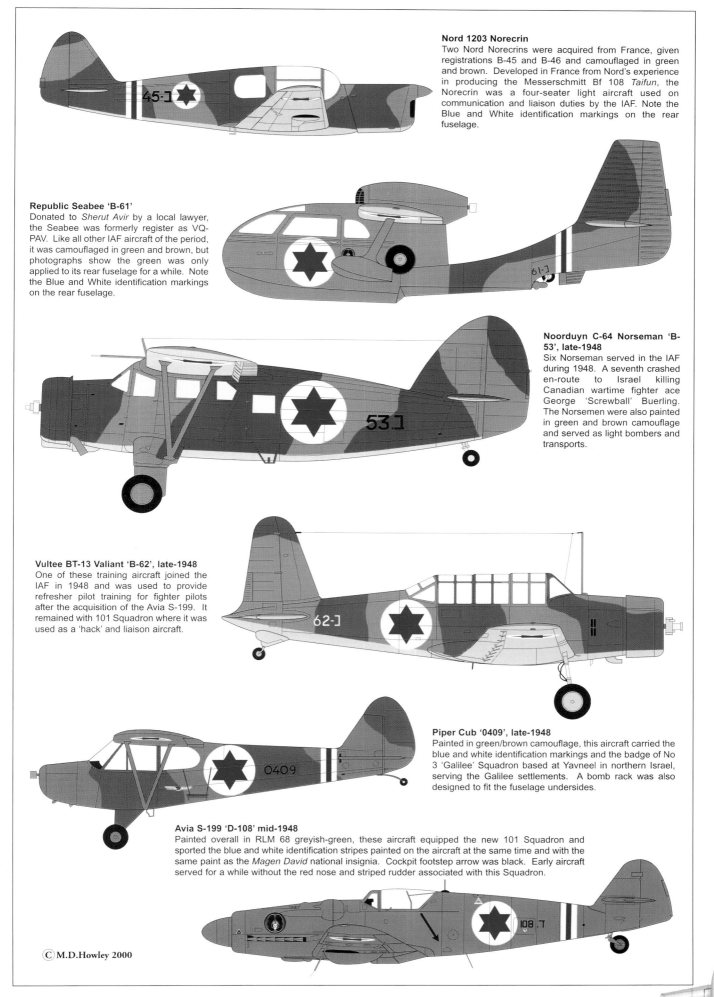

Nord 1203 Norecrin

Two Nord Norecrins were acquired from France, given registrations B-45 and B-46 and camouflaged in green and brown. Developed in France from Nord's experience in producing the Messerschmitt Bf 108 *Taifun*, the Norecrin was a four-seater light aircraft used on communication and liaison duties by the IAF. Note the Blue and White identification markings on the rear fuselage.

Republic Seabee 'B-61'

Donated to *Sherut Avir* by a local lawyer, the Seabee was formerly register as VQ-PAV. Like all other IAF aircraft of the period, it was camouflaged in green and brown, but photographs show the green was only applied to its rear fuselage for a while. Note the Blue and White identification markings on the rear fuselage.

Noorduyn C-64 Norseman 'B-53', late-1948

Six Norseman served in the IAF during 1948. A seventh crashed en-route to Israel killing Canadian wartime fighter ace George 'Screwball' Buerling. The Norsemen were also painted in green and brown camouflage and served as light bombers and transports.

Vultee BT-13 Valiant 'B-62', late-1948

One of these training aircraft joined the IAF in 1948 and was used to provide refresher pilot training for fighter pilots after the acquisition of the Avia S-199. It remained with 101 Squadron where it was used as a 'hack' and liaison aircraft.

Piper Cub '0409', late-1948

Painted in green/brown camouflage, this aircraft carried the blue and white identification markings and the badge of No 3 'Galilee' Squadron based at Yavneel in northern Israel, serving the Galilee settlements. A bomb rack was also designed to fit the fuselage undersides.

Avia S-199 'D-108' mid-1948

Painted overall in RLM 68 greyish-green, these aircraft equipped the new 101 Squadron and sported the blue and white identification markings and stripes painted on the aircraft at the same time and with the same paint as the *Magen David* national insignia. Cockpit footstep arrow was black. Early aircraft served for a while without the red nose and striped rudder associated with this Squadron.

© M.D.Howley 2000

to support the outlying settlements as best they could, ferrying essential supplies.

In December 1947, most of the aircraft and their related equipment and personnel were formed into the *Sherut Avir*, *Haganah* Air Arm, and from then on their activities formed part of the national defence effort. Aviron continued to operate, linking closely with the Arms Purchasing Group, (Rekhesh), tasked to acquire aircraft as part of Operation 'Yukum Purkan', (Salvation from the Skies).

The first action of the *Sherut Avir* was to move their aircraft at Lydda Airport, which was enclosed by Arabs in Ramle and Lydda town. Permission was given for Aviron to open the old Tel Aviv Airfield, unused since early World War Two, and work progressed to make the airfield operational to accept the *Sherut Avir* aircraft from Lydda. The airfield was given the name Sde Dov (Dov Field) after a Chairman of Aviron, Mr Dov Hoz.

Sherut Avir assets

At the start, the *Sherut Avir* assets were:

Taylorcraft BL	VQ-PAI
Taylorcraft BL	VQ-PAJ
RWD 13	VQ-PAL
RWD 13	VQ-PAM
DH-82C Tiger Moth	VQ-PAT
DH-82C Tiger Moth	VQ-PAU
Auster J1 Autocrat	VQ-PAS
Dragon Rapide	VQ-PAR

The Tiger Moths were acquired by the Aero Club during 1947 and the Autocrat by Aviron in 1946. Other aircraft which had served the *Haganah* but which did not become assets of *Sherut Avir* include:
• Miles M3A Falcon VQ-PAO acquired by Aviron in 1940 and sold to the US Ambassador to Cairo.

• Benes-Mraz Be-550 Bibi VQ-PAQ acquired by Aviron in 1942, but crashed in November 1947
• Zlin XII, VQ-PAP operated in Palestine by the right-wing *Irgun* organisation.

As the scale of the conflict increased, it quickly became apparent that the number of aircraft available was inadequate for the task ahead. Supplying the beleaguered settlements was a high priority, but if the fighting escalated supply missions would not be enough. There would be a need for offensive support, a role for which none of the aircraft had been designed. Never the less, the light aircraft were proving their worth, slipping in and out of landing strips, delivering supplies, weapons and ammunition and evacuating the wounded. When Aviron heard the British Government were offering for sale twenty ex-Army Observation Auster light aircraft for an asking price of £14,000.00, they wasted no opportunity and bought all twenty for the *Sherut Avir*, quickly spiriting them away into hiding, before the true identity of the new owners was discovered and the deal reneged upon.

Over the next few month the Austers were re-assembled, brought up to flying condition and entered service. The batch comprised two Auster Mk 3s with 130 hp Gypsy Major engines and eighteen Auster Mk 5s with the 130 hp Lycoming engine. As these aircraft had all been purchased clandestinely for the *Sherut Avir*, they could not be officially registered, instead, they were given the same registration letters of the legitimate aircraft and painted the yellow, or silver dope colour of the Aviron Tailorcrafts! Several times, discovery was only averted by quick thinking pilots as they came into land on official airfields and saw an identically registered aircraft already on

the field !

Aviron also delivered its DH Rapide, VQ-PAC alongside the Austers and two other aircraft joined the inventory in unusual circumstances.

A lawyer donated a Republic Seabee amphibian VQ-PAV and *Haganah* soldiers patrolling the Negev desert in the south discovered the Fairchild F-24R Argus of an Egyptian smuggler and commandeered it into service. This was given the registration VQ-PAM, the same as an RWD 13.

The arrival of these additional aircraft enabled the *Sherut Avir* to organise its air assets into squadrons and locate them where they would do the most good. The organisation became:-

Number 1 Squadron, based at Sde Dov to meet the needs of the Central Command and provide communication and supply support for the Tel-Aviv-Jerusalem areas.

Number 2 Squadron, located near the Southern Command Headquarters of the *Haganah* 'Negev' Brigade at Kibbutz Nir-Am, where a dirt runway had been hastily constructed to enable the aircraft to support the twenty-three Kibbutz Settlements scattered over a wide area.

Number 3 Squadron, located on a field near Yavniel, South West of the Sea of Galilee, next to the Headquarters of the 'Golani' Brigade. From here the Squadron could support the Northern Jewish Town communities and Settlements.

Number 4 Squadron was added later, located at Sde Dov to assist with the central operations including supply missions to the increasingly isolated community in Jerusalem, which was becoming impossible to reach by road.

Whilst all this was happening, the need for offensive aircraft had not been overlooked. As the fighting intensified many of the light aircraft were modified to perform attack functions. Armed with a machine gun in the cockpit to fire through an open door or window and with improvised fittings for bombs or hand-grenades, the aircraft flew many missions, often proving vital in breaking a heavy Arab attack. However, the *Haganah* knew that the impending declaration of Independence, would lead to an attack by the regular Armed Forces of the neighbouring Arab Nations and aircraft would be needed to compete with them on equal terms, otherwise they would not survive.

Enter the 'Mule'
In December 1947 the Arms Purchasing Group found the Government of Czechoslovakia willing to supply arms in exchange for much needed American Dollars. Orders for all types of arms were given and aircraft chartered from the United States to deliver them to the *Haganah* in Palestine. Part of the

Above: One of the twenty Austers purchased by Aviran for use by the *Sherut Avir* in January 1948. This Auster AOP 5 is also in the 'brown and green' camouflage hurredly applied during May 1948.

Below: This Fairchild Argus was captured by *Haganah* soldiers on patrol in the Negev Desert where it was being used by an Egyptian smuggler. Pressed in to *Sherut Avir* service, first in the fictitious registration VQ-PAM, it was then camouflaged in 'green and brown' with grey undersides. Its IAF service serial was B-30, changing to 0501 in November 1948.

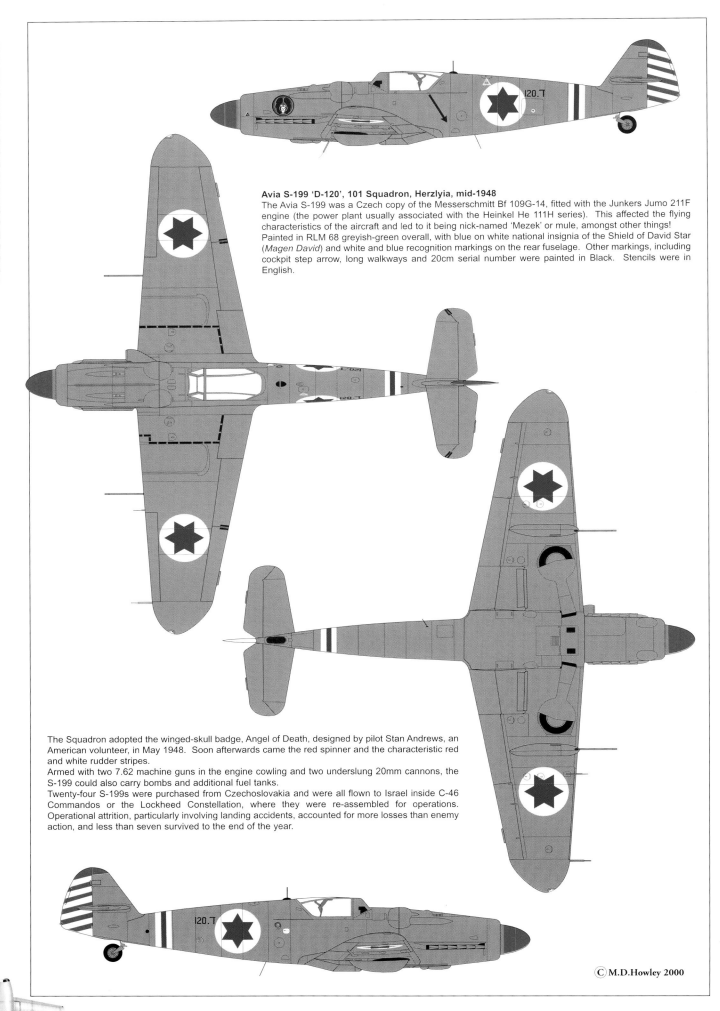

Avia S-199 'D-120', 101 Squadron, Herzlyia, mid-1948
The Avia S-199 was a Czech copy of the Messerschmitt Bf 109G-14, fitted with the Junkers Jumo 211F engine (the power plant usually associated with the Heinkel He 111H series). This affected the flying characteristics of the aircraft and led to it being nick-named 'Mezek' or mule, amongst other things!
Painted in RLM 68 greyish-green overall, with blue on white national insignia of the Shield of David Star (*Magen David*) and white and blue recognition markings on the rear fuselage. Other markings, including cockpit step arrow, long walkways and 20cm serial number were painted in Black. Stencils were in English.

The Squadron adopted the winged-skull badge, Angel of Death, designed by pilot Stan Andrews, an American volunteer, in May 1948. Soon afterwards came the red spinner and the characteristic red and white rudder stripes.
Armed with two 7.62 machine guns in the engine cowling and two underslung 20mm cannons, the S-199 could also carry bombs and additional fuel tanks.
Twenty-four S-199s were purchased from Czechoslovakia and were all flown to Israel inside C-46 Commandos or the Lockheed Constellation, where they were re-assembled for operations. Operational attrition, particularly involving landing accidents, accounted for more losses than enemy action, and less than seven survived to the end of the year.

© M.D.Howley 2000

discussions with the Czech Authorities related to the supply of fighter aircraft and to the delight of the negotiators, a deal was concluded in April 1948 for the delivery of ten Avia S-199 single seat fighters.

The Avia Aircraft Factory in Czechoslovakia had been taken over by the Germans in World War Two for the production of Messerschmitt Bf 109 fighters. The Avia S-199 was the Czech version of one of the latest variants produced, the Bf 109G-14. In producing the fighter for the new Czech Air Force, Avia had to overcome a serious problem

when their engine plant was destroyed by fire and the normal Daimler Benz DB 605 power plant was not available for the fighter.

Avia, not to be daunted by this, had a number of Junkers Jumo 211F engines, originally destined for Heinkel He 111H bombers available to them, and at 1350 hp, these were deemed suitable replacement engines for the S-199 fighter. It was not a marriage made in heaven as this engine was heavier and produced less power, which altered the centre of gravity and added some very difficult handling characteristics. The

Above: Piper Cub, 0409, formerly A-58, of the Third Squadron 'Galilee' whose badge is painted under the cockpit. These aircraft operated out of Yavneil and Ramat David in Northern Israel.

Below: Three pilots of 101 Sqn pose alongside one of their Avia S-199s in the summer of 1948. Of note is the 'winged skull' squadron badge painted on the left side of the engine cowling.

Above: One of two Nord Norecrins that were acquired, F-BEUI and F-BEUH, showing to good effect the white/blue/white recognition markings painted around the rear fuselage. They served in the IAF as B-45 and B-46.

Left: Miles Aerovan, B-71, operated as an Air Ambulance out of Sde Dov airfield. On 17 July 1948, it made a forced landing on the coastal flats south of Jaffa, and its pilot set off to find help. On his return with a rescue party, he found that the aircraft had been destroyed and all the occupants killed or wounded by Arab irregular soldiers.

Below: Three Beech Bonanzas were acquired for the IAF, two from South Africa and one from the UK. The un-numbered aircraft in this photograph, was originally delivered in natural metal with a red nose and fuselage stripes. The IAF crudely applied a thin coat of brown and green camouflage paint over this.

Above: An Avia S-199, at the Israeli Air Force Museum at Hatzerim, was restored as D-120 in the mid-1990s. This aircraft was repainted in the markings and correct RLM 68 shade it would have been finished in whilst operating in the war of Independence in 1948.

Left: One of the embryo Israeli Air Force 's first pilots, Ezer Weizman, centre, with two other 101 Sqn pilots infront of an Avia S-199. The Avia was called *Mezek* (Mule) because of its difficult handling characteristics, and many were damaged through landing accidents.

Below: An Avia S-199 of 101 Sqn., based at Herzliya in the summer of 1948, with Ezer Weizman taking a close look at the 101 Sqn 'winged skull' badge. Note the two other Avias in the background. At this time, the rudders of the aircraft had not been painted with the red and white diagonal stripes and the spinners were still in the RLM 68 greyish-green of the rest of the airframe. Ezer Weizman, an ex-RAF pilot, is the current President of the State of Israel.

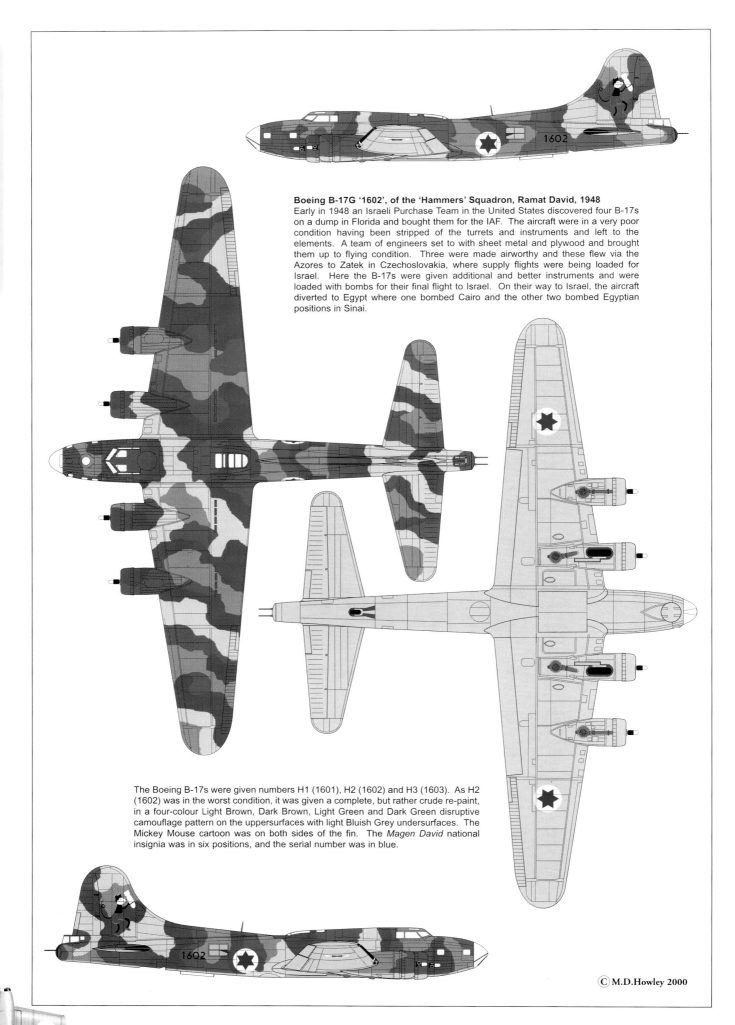

Boeing B-17G '1602', of the 'Hammers' Squadron, Ramat David, 1948
Early in 1948 an Israeli Purchase Team in the United States discovered four B-17s on a dump in Florida and bought them for the IAF. The aircraft were in a very poor condition having been stripped of the turrets and instruments and left to the elements. A team of engineers set to with sheet metal and plywood and brought them up to flying condition. Three were made airworthy and these flew via the Azores to Zatek in Czechoslovakia, where supply flights were being loaded for Israel. Here the B-17s were given additional and better instruments and were loaded with bombs for their final flight to Israel. On their way to Israel, the aircraft diverted to Egypt where one bombed Cairo and the other two bombed Egyptian positions in Sinai.

The Boeing B-17s were given numbers H1 (1601), H2 (1602) and H3 (1603). As H2 (1602) was in the worst condition, it was given a complete, but rather crude re-paint, in a four-colour Light Brown, Dark Brown, Light Green and Dark Green disruptive camouflage pattern on the uppersurfaces with light Bluish Grey undersurfaces. The Mickey Mouse cartoon was on both sides of the fin. The *Magen David* national insignia was in six positions, and the serial number was in blue.

© M.D.Howley 2000

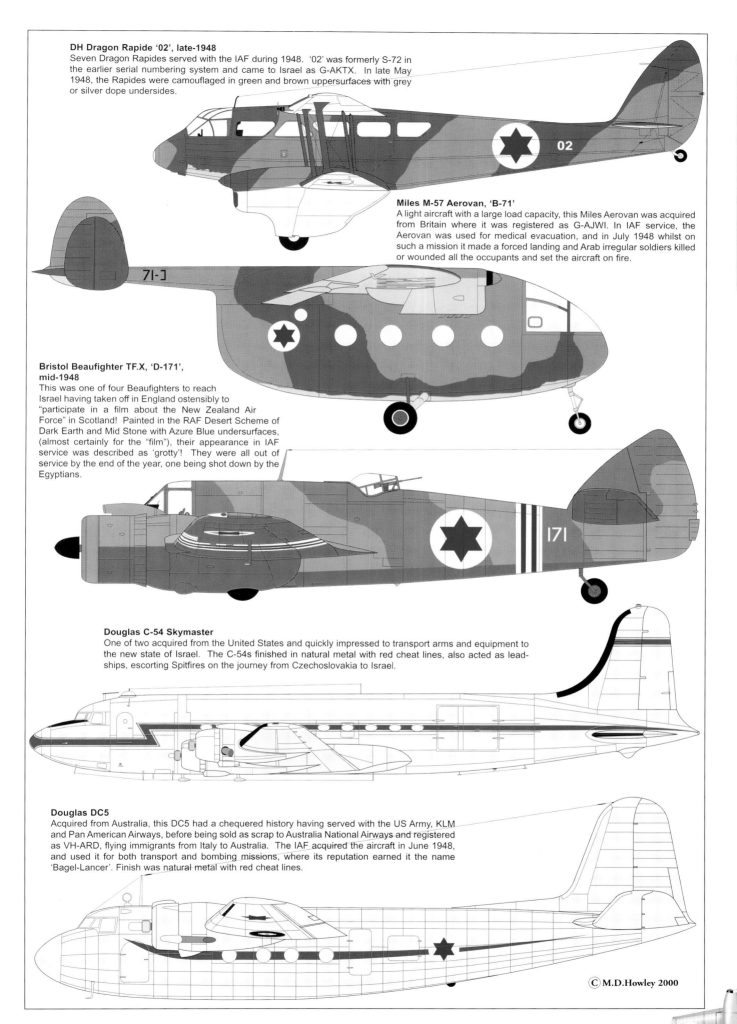

DH Dragon Rapide '02', late-1948
Seven Dragon Rapides served with the IAF during 1948. '02' was formerly S-72 in the earlier serial numbering system and came to Israel as G-AKTX. In late May 1948, the Rapides were camouflaged in green and brown uppersurfaces with grey or silver dope undersides.

Miles M-57 Aerovan, 'B-71'
A light aircraft with a large load capacity, this Miles Aerovan was acquired from Britain where it was registered as G-AJWI. In IAF service, the Aerovan was used for medical evacuation, and in July 1948 whilst on such a mission it made a forced landing and Arab irregular soldiers killed or wounded all the occupants and set the aircraft on fire.

Bristol Beaufighter TF.X, 'D-171', mid-1948
This was one of four Beaufighters to reach Israel having taken off in England ostensibly to "participate in a film about the New Zealand Air Force" in Scotland! Painted in the RAF Desert Scheme of Dark Earth and Mid Stone with Azure Blue undersurfaces, (almost certainly for the "film"), their appearance in IAF service was described as 'grotty'! They were all out of service by the end of the year, one being shot down by the Egyptians.

Douglas C-54 Skymaster
One of two acquired from the United States and quickly impressed to transport arms and equipment to the new state of Israel. The C-54s finished in natural metal with red cheat lines, also acted as lead-ships, escorting Spitfires on the journey from Czechoslovakia to Israel.

Douglas DC5
Acquired from Australia, this DC5 had a chequered history having served with the US Army, KLM and Pan American Airways, before being sold as scrap to Australia National Airways and registered as VH-ARD, flying immigrants from Italy to Australia. The IAF acquired the aircraft in June 1948, and used it for both transport and bombing missions, where its reputation earned it the name 'Bagel-Lancer'. Finish was natural metal with red cheat lines.

© M.D.Howley 2000

Above: Another Fairchild Argus - one of three that arrived from South Africa, registered ZS-BBB, ZS-BBC and ZS-BBD, landing in Palestine on 9 May 1948. They served in the IAF and were given the serial numbers, B-31, B-32 and B-33.

aircraft became known as the *'Mezek'* (Mule) because of these characteristics, the worst being a tendency to swing away from its straight course when power was applied, a dangerous trait on take-off with the narrow track undercarriage associated with the Messerschmitt fighter.

A flying school had been established in secrecy in Italy, near Rome (Alicia), and from there and Palestine, crews were selected and sent to Czechoslovakia for two weeks training on type. This included full conversion training and tactical training, getting to know the capabilities of the fighter armed with 2 x 20mm cannon and 2 x 13.2mm machine guns with racks for carrying bombs. The deal with Czechoslovakia also included ammunition and bombs and once delivery to Israel was underway the order was increased from ten to twenty-five aircraft. The confirmation of this deal meant all the efforts were concentrated on seeing it through, which also meant the termination of discussions with Mexico about the sale of twenty-five P-47D Thunderbolts. Oh, what might have been!

The first aircraft were flown to Israel in a chartered Douglas C-54 Skymaster, but April 1948 also saw aircraft purchases in the United States come to fruition and soon Curtiss C-46 Commandos and Lockheed C-69 Constellations joined in the airlift of arms. It was over 11 hours flying time from Zatec in Czechoslovakia to the former RAF airfield at Ekron in Palestine, now taken over by *Sherut Avir* and renamed Tel-Nof.

The first Avia S-199s were delivered on 20 May 1948 and were quickly

Right: Prime Minister, David Ben-Gurion, and his wife, visiting 101 Sqn at Natanya in August 1948. 101 Squadron's Commander, Modi Alon (in sunglasses) is standing next to the Prime Minister. Note the DH Dragon Rapide in the background.

assembled for action by the engineers of the newly formed 101 Squadron, the first fighter squadron. It is now known that they were painted overall in RLM 68, a greyish-green colour. The Avia Factory in Czechoslovakia which built the Bf 109s for the *Luftwaffe* in World War Two still had plenty of parts and paint stocks left over. Identification stripes on the rear fuselage were white/blue/white, with the blue and white being the same colours as the national insignia and added at the same time. When time permitted, the rudder was painted in red and white diagonal lines, which was to become standard for this Squadron.

May 1948 also saw the delivery of other aircraft types into the inventory, including two Beechcraft Bonanzas and a Douglas C-47 Dakota from South Africa. To increase procurement of suitable aircraft, Sherat Avir pilot Boris Senior,

was asked to return to his native South Africa to recruit volunteers, and acquire more aircraft. He was immediately successful, and in early 1948, had acquired two Beech Bonanzas, ZS-BTE and ZS-BWS, three Fairchild Arguses, ZS-BBB, ZS-BBC and ZS-BBD, and several Dakotas, including ZS-AVI, ZS-AVM, ZS-AVK and ZS-DCZ.

In early 1948, members of the Purchasing Team, posing as representatives of a Belgian Airline managed to secure delivery of twenty former US Army C-64 Norseman Utility Transports. The first three aircraft flew via Rome which was the last refuelling stop before flying on to Israel. Unfortunately, after take off on the afternoon of 20 May, one of the aircraft was seen to explode and crash into the sea killing its pilot, George 'Screwball' Buerling, the Canadian wartime fighter ace who, like

Above: Curtiss C-46 Commando '138' of 106 Transport Squadron, circa 1948. This particular aircraft was acquired from the United States and registered with the Panamanian airline LAPSA as RX-138. For service in the Israeli Air Force, it received an uppersurface camouflage of 'Olive Green', but retained its natural metal undersides. The number '138' was kept.

Right: Close-up view of '138's nose showing the name *Shosh* (short for *Shoshana*) written in Hebrew below the cockpit window. Note how 'roughly' the camouflage paint was applied by brush.

Below: Pan African Airways Douglas DC3 Dakota, ZS-AVK, leased in South Africa to assist with the transport of arms and equipment. It arrived in Palestine in April 1948, and later served in the IAF as transport S-83, before crashing in flames on 25 October 1948, when landing at Tel Nof airfield. Unfortunately, all on board were killed, including the captain, Wilf Canter, who had gained a DFM when flying for RAF Bomber Command. Note the Miles Gemini, G-AKEP in the background

Above: Noorduyn Norseman '0802', formerly B-53, flew many supply missions, transporting men and vital stores throughout Israel. Following a landing accident on 28 December 1948, it sustained severe damage and was taken out of service.

many others was making his way to Israel to volunteer himself to their cause. The reason for the crash was attributed to sabotage.

On 14 May 1948, with the ending of the British Mandate, the creation of the new State of Israel was declared by David Ben Gurion on the lines of partition agreed by the United Nations. This declaration was immediately followed by an attack by forces of the Arab League. On 27 May, *Sherut Avir* became the official Israeli Defence Forces/ Air Force (*Chel Ha'Avir*) under the command of Major-General Aharon Ramez, a former wartime RAF Sergeant Pilot.

A hard start in life

The day after Ben Gurion's declaration of Statehood, Egyptian Air Force Spitfires attacked Sde Dov Airfield damaging a hangar and several of the aircraft. From then on the light aircraft were camouflaged, usually in dark green and earth brown uppersurfaces using paint mixed from stocks left behind by the RAF.

There was no standardisation on a camouflage pattern, nor on the actual colours, so several shades of browns and greens existed, including the actual RAF shades of Dark Green and Dark Earth. The Transport Aircraft, Dakotas, C-46 Commandos and Dragon Rapides also acquired camouflage paintwork, again without any standardisation.

The intervention of the armies of the Arab League meant no respite for the aircraft and personnel of the IAF. Preparing for war, each aircraft was made ready for its allocated role and location. A hasty programme of camouflaging the aircraft was instigated. With no standard camouflage patterns or colour schemes, and with IAF ground crews obtaining paint from so many different sources and suppliers, including household and agricultural paints, it is difficult to be pedantic about the actual colour of any individual aeroplane. As mentioned previously, stocks of standard RAF paint left at their former airfields and depots were put to good use. In many cases it is only the memories of air and ground crews that can provide any colour reference, but it is known that shades of green and brown predominated, often applied in crude brush strokes.

Worsening situation

The situation became serious on all fronts, and every effort was made to get the Avia S-199s into action as soon as they could be assembled and readied. In the South, an Egyptian Expeditionary force attacked from Gaza and began to overwhelm the hard pressed Israeli defenders. When this force reached Ashdod, just 17 miles from Tel Aviv, air support was urgently requested. The air and ground crews of 101 Squadron were having a busy time - first, assembling the aircraft and second, trying to meet all the demands made upon them.

The priority they had been given was the defence of Tel Aviv which was being regularly bombed by the Egyptian Air Force. The answer to this was a planned strike against the Egyptians based at El Arish in Sinai. On 29 May 1948, as the aircraft were being readied for this strike, Egyptian Spitfires attacked Tel-Nof, destroying a hangar containing unassembled Avias and some spare parts. However, the four Avias assigned for the strike were untouched and just as they were about to take off, the IAF Command changed their plans ordering a strike on the Egyptian Force at Ashdod.

As dusk fell, the Avias came out of the setting sun bombing and shooting, completely taking the Force by surprise. The attack proved decisive and the demoralised Egyptians made no further advances, eventually withdrawing to their own territory. It was not all one sided however, the IAF lost two of the Avias to ground fire, one over the battlefield and the other crashing on landing as a result

Left: A Beech Bonanza shown carrying a bomb on the locally designed and fitted bomb rack. On 4 June 1948, a Beech Bonanza participated in the bombing of an Egyptian Troopship, *Amira Fauzia* and its supporting vessels as they headed towards Tel Avi.

of damage sustained. An attrition rate of 50% on their first mission!

The next day saw a repeat of this action as the two remaining Avias were sent to attack an Iraqi Armoured Column which had penetrated central Israel and threatened to split the country in two as it reached Tul Karn less than 10 miles from the coast between Tel Aviv and Haifa. Again the attack was successful, but again another aircraft was lost in action maintaining the 50% attrition.

As Modi Alon's action over Tel Aviv was to prove, this attrition rate was turned, but rarely were there more than four or five aircraft available at any one time.

On 1 June 1948, the Council of the Arab League met in Jordan's capital Amman, to discuss a United Nations Cease-fire proposal, something which the pressured Israelis were keen to accept. The IAF became instrumental in influencing the outcome by launching a couple of audacious bombing raids.

During the night of the 2 June, two DH Rapides armed with bombs, and a single Bren Gun in the doorway for self defence, took off from Sde Dov and headed for Amman. They meet with no anti-aircraft fire over a lit up city and successfully bombed their targets near the Arab league meeting hall.

On 4 June 1948, an Egyptian Naval Convoy comprising the Troopship *Amira Fauzia* together with a Landing Craft and an escorting Frigate were seen heading towards Tel Aviv. During the afternoon the convoy was attacked by a DH Rapide, a Beech Bonanza and a Fairchild Argus, all equipped with bombs held on improvised racks. Only one hit was made, and because of the intensive return fire the Argus was hit and lost, killing its crew. However, in the face of such a determined attack, the Egyptian Convoy steamed away.

On 9 June 1948, two Avia 199s from 101 Squadron, flown by Modi Alon and Gidi Lichtman, on patrol south of Tel Aviv, spotted four Egyptian Air Force Spitfires heading towards the city. The Avias entered a dogfight with the Spitfires, with Gidi gaining the upper hand in his fight, shooting one down into the sea. This was the first fighter-versus-fighter victory for the IAF and the first time Spitfires and 'Messerschmitts' had clashed since World War Two. The following day a lone IAF Dakota dropped two tons of bombs on the Syrian capital Damascus, bringing home again the capability of the IAF.

On 11 June 1948, the United Nations' sponsored cease-fire came into effect, giving the tired combatants a welcome respite. Israel had become an independent country, but only controlled one third of the land allocated in the United Nations Partition Agreement. This was the first of several cease-fires in a bitter dispute that was to end in June 1949.

More badly needed aircraft and foreign volunteer crews, many non-Jewish, continued to arrive in Israel as overseas purchasing and recruitment missions became more successful as Israel became a recognised State. The IAF took advantage of the cease-fire to reorganise itself and make use of the facilities left to them when the RAF finally gave up its bases in Palestine.

In June 1948, 101 Squadron moved from Tel-Nof to a field at Hertzelia, north of Tel-Aviv. A landing strip was prepared on the agricultural settlement, with farm buildings used to shelter the aircraft which could also be hidden amongst the orchards. This afforded better protection than Tel-Nof which was also becoming increasingly busy, accommodating C-46 Commandos and other Transport Aircraft and the Southern Light Aircraft Squadron which had expanded its aircraft numbers but had to move from its Negev locations because of the hostilities. A further transport base was established on the former RAF base at Ramat David to operate Douglas C-47 Dakotas, and a single Douglas DC-5, which became known as the 'Bagel Lancer'.

Many of the transport types including the Curtiss C-46 Commandos and the Lockheed C-69 Constellation arrived in Israel after perilous journeys via South America and North Africa. They were originally bought for a fictitious Panamanian Airline called 'Lineas Aereas de Panama SA' (LAPSA) and actually registered in Panama with RX registration codes.

Ramat David was also to become the home of the heavy bomber squadron when three Boeing B-17G Flying Fortresses were acquired from the USA. Their journey to Israel was equally adventurous.

Bigger bombers

The Purchasing Team in the United States led by Al Schwimmer had been successful in obtaining the transport aircraft, but when the four Flying Fortresses were discovered for sale on a dump in Florida, they knew these would be welcome additions to the IAF inventory. The aircraft were in a poor condition, the gun turrets had been removed along with a lot of equipment and instruments. A team of engineers salvaged and repaired what they could, filling in turret holes with plywood and sheet metal, gradually bringing them upto flying condition.

Volunteer crews were found under the command of Ray Kurtz, a former USAAF B-17 Captain and the aircraft took off for Brazil. However this flight plan was a ruse, and the true destination was Zatec in Czechoslovakia which they reached via Puerto Rico and the Azores. At Zatec, the aircraft were given further repairs, some more instruments were found including wartime *Luftwaffe* bomb-sights and the Czechs supplied some 500lb bombs. The B-17s were ready for war.

On 15 July 1948, the B-17s left Zatec for Israel, but the route had been planned in order to carry out a bombing mission over Egypt on the way. In retaliation for Egyptian raids on Israel, the B-17s were to attack targets in Cairo, Gaza and El-Arish. Kurtz led the formation over Austria encountering dangerous flying conditions and on down the coast of Yugoslavia and Albania where they were subject to anti-aircraft fire. Over Crete, the formation split with each aircraft going to its allotted target. In the lead B-17, Kurtz headed for Cairo which was lit up like a beacon. They bombed the target and headed towards Israel without a shot being fired at them. The other two B-17s bombed troop concentrations. All the aircraft landed safely at Ekron on completing their missions. The other B-17s had joined up and bombed troop concentrations at Gaza when the E-Arish target could not be identified. They all landed safely at Ekron. When the War for Independence ended, the B-17s had flown over 200 missions, playing a major role in the breaking Egyptian attacks form Gaza and Sinai. With these new bombers came some new fighters.

Spitfires

The Israeli Purchasing Team in Czechoslovakia heard that the Czech Government were willing to sell its Spitfires Mk IXs originally supplied by Britain. A deal was signed to supply Israel with fifty Spitfire LF Mk IXes, most with clipped wings. Later a further nine aircraft were added to the order. However, these were not the first Spitfires in IAF service.

On 15 May 1948, an Egyptian Air Force Spitfire attacking Sde Dov airfield was hit by ground fire and crash landed on the shore near Hertzelia. Although badly damaged, it was salvaged and taken to Ma'arborot in the north of Tel Aviv where an engineering workshop was established. When the RAF withdrew from Palestine, it left behind a considerable amount of spares and equipment, not to mention junkyards, with those at Ein-Shemer and Ekron proving very resourceful. The Egyptian Spitfire together with parts from Ein-Shemer, enabled an airworthy Spitfire to be assembled. Later, parts from other Egyptian Spitfires shot down by the RAF after the Egyptian Air Force had attacked them at Ramat David, thinking the base was occupied by the Israelis, were also salvaged and brought to the workshop. By October 1948 the IAF had four operational Spitfires numbered D-130 - 133, and allocated to 101 Squadron.

Participating in many ground operations, they scored their first air-to-air victory on 21 October when Jack Doyle, a Canadian Volunteer and former war ace flying in Spitfire D-132, shot down an Egyptian Spitfire over the Negev. Spitfire D-130 was also configured for photo-reconnaissance and performed many missions in this role over the region.

With the Czech Spitfires based at Kunovice, it was too far for a direct ferry flight to Israel and the these aircraft would not easily fit inside the transport aircraft like the Avias. An Israeli engineer, Sam Pomerance, came up with the solution. Stripping the Spitfires down in weight and fitting them with a belly

Above: Danny Shapira, later to become Chief Test Pilot for Israel Aircraft Industries, dons his parachute for a mission in Spitfire '12' in early 1949.

Left: Another photograph in the sequence, showing Danny Shapira about to enter the cockpit. Of note is the badly weathered appearance of the aircraft - operational needs were more important than looks at this time.

slipper tank and ex-*Luftwaffe* 300ltr wing tanks, would increase their range sufficiently enough to make it in two 'hops'. Agreement was reached with the Yugoslavian Authorities for use of an airfield at Podgorica in the south, and 'Operation Velveta' was launched to get these much need fighters to Israel. On 24 September 1948, six Spitfires took off, led by Sam Pomerance, and made it to Yugoslavia, where unfortunately, one was damaged on landing. On 27 September, the remaining five, took off, escorted by a Douglas C-54, for the long over water 'hop' to Israel, but it did not go to plan.

The Spitfires being flown by Modi Alon and Boris Senior developed fuel problems and they made emergency landings in Greece, both pilots were held for a month before being released, but their aircraft were impounded. The other three Spitfires arrived safely at Ramat David.

Following this exercise, ten Spitfires were dismantled, crated and sent to Israel by a tortuous road and sea journey. This was a lengthy process and in December 1948, 'Operation Velveta II' was launched to resume the deliveries by air. Between 19 - 26 December 1948, twelve Spitfires made it to Israel in flights escorted by C-46 Commandos. Sadly, at the start of the operation Sam Pomerance was killed when his aircraft

Above and at right: Spitfire D-130 - a Spitfire of many parts, as can be seen from the engine cowling panels. The RAF left behind a number of aircraft dumps at Ein-Shemer, Ekron and Ramat David, which were scoured for aircraft parts. These parts, together with parts salvaged from shot down Egyptian Spitfires enabled the IAF to re-build five Spitfires. D-130, also had provision to carry a camera and performed many photo reconnaissance missions. It was painted in green primer.

crashed in a severe snow storm. The IAF received fifty-six of the fifty-nine Spitfires ordered, and all were delivered by the end of 1949, most having been sent by sea. Those delivered by air proved crucial in affecting the outcome of the fighting being re-equipped for combat as soon as they arrived. On 28 December 1948, Jack Doyle scored the second Spitfire air-to-air victory, shooting down an Egyptian Macchi MC 205V over Faluja on the southern front. Other Spitfire victories were to follow.

Apart from the first re-built Spitfires acquired, which were painted in a dark green primer, the Spitfires from Czechoslovakia were still painted in the standard wartime RAF Day Fighter scheme of Ocean Grey and Dark Green uppersurfaces with Medium Sea Grey undersurfaces. Identification stripes of white/blue/white were painted under the wings only, at the request of the Army who preferred this to the fuselage stripes on the Avias and the earlier acquired Spitfires.

Right: Another one of the original five Spitfire Mk IXs, assembled from crashed aircraft parts and spares left behind in maintenace sites in Israel by their former RAF occupants. These aircraft were given serial numbers D-130 to D-134, This particular Spitfire, in 101 Sqn service circa early 1948, is fitted with a c wing, differentiating it from the e wing Mk IXs acquired from Czechoslovakia.

More reinforcements

At the same time as the Spitfires deliveries were under way, other aircraft procurement efforts were also successful. From the United States came seventeen North American AT-6 Harvards and four North American P-51D Mustangs. Both were soon in action, the Harvards particularly useful as light bombers. From Britain came four Bristol Beaufighters although their purchase was far from normal.

Early in 1948, a film company R Dickson and Partners, put a proposal together for a documentary on the Royal New Zealand Air Force and bought five Beaufighters to feature in the film. A

Right and below: A superbly refurbished Spitfire Mk IXe on display at the IAF Museum at Hatzor, painted-up to represent 2011 '26' of 101 Sqn., circa late 1948 in the Dark Green, Ocean Grey and Medium Sea Grey scheme. This Spitfire was originally one of the 'Velveta II' aircraft acquired from Czechoslovakia.

Left: Curtiss C-46 Commando of 106 Transport Squadron, still in its original overall natural metal finish, receiving some maintenance to its nose. These aircraft flew many vital missions, including transporting Avia S-199s from Czechoslovakia to Israel.

flight plan was filed for a journey to Scotland, chosen because it had similar scenery to that found in New Zealand. The Beaufighters, stripped of all armament, took off for Scotland but strangely never arrived. They were next heard of when four of them turned up for refuelling in Corsica. One of the Beaufighters had unfortunately crashed at Thame in Oxfordshire on 28 July 1948, killing its pilot.

The surviving four aircraft, (RD135, RD448, RD427 and LZ185), all made it to Israel where, to help serviceability LZ185 became a 'hangar-queen' as a source of spare parts. The man called R Dickson turned out to be Emmanuel Zur, acting on behalf of Rekesh, and he had been particularly successful. Not only had he acquired the aircraft but he also

acquired full armament fits and additional spare parts. Using his connections he chartered an HP Halifax Mk VIII Transport, and captained by an Israeli ex-RAF Pilot, the fully laden Halifax took off for Israel. Bad luck set in on their arrival as they approached Ekron late at night, to find it in total darkness. As their fuel state became critical, they flew to Tel Aviv and made an emergency landing, crashing off the end of the short runway. However, the cargo and crew survived.

The Beaufighters, were given IAF serials D-170 - 173, and had a short but hectic existence in IAF service. Arriving in August 1948 they were in action by the end of the month, attacking Egyptian positions in the South. Their story is inevitably linked with that of Len Fitchet, a non-Jewish volunteer, who had served with the Royal Canadian Air Force and who was responsible for scoring the very last aerial victory over the *Luftwaffe*. Len made the Beaufighter his own, his skilful flying led to the crash of an Iraqi Hawker Fury which tried to intercept him.

However, on 23 October 1948, whilst attacking the Egyptian Fort at Iraq-Suweidan, his Beaufighter was hit and crash landed nearby. Len, at just 25 years old, and his crew member were killed in the crash.

By December 1948, their workload began to take toll and the lack of spares had grounded the remaining Beaufighters. The paintwork on these Beaufighters has been described as 'well worn', with the original RAF Dark Earth, Mid Stone and Azure Blue desert scheme colours fading off and the aircraft receiving local 'touching-up' which did not enhance their appearance. The blue and white fuselage and wing identification stripes were also added before they participated in combat.

Cease fire

The War of Independence came to an end with the acceptance of a cease-fire in January 1949. By that time, major Israeli initiatives such as 'Operation Hirem' in the North and Operations 'Yoav' and 'Chorev' in the South, which had all been supported by numerous ground attack missions by the IAF, had been successful in defending the State and establishing air superiority over its territory and beyond the battle fronts. International pressure, particularly from Britain, which had a Defence Treaty with Egypt for the protection of the Suez Canal, forced the Israelis to stop pursuing the Egyptians into Sinai and for all sides to accept a cease fire and begin talks to resolve the conflict, ending the

current fighting. The IAF had faced its first test, but had relied heavily on Foreign Volunteers, 'The Mahal' who accounted for nearly two thirds of the pilots. At the end of the war, most of these volunteers returned to their homelands and the IAF would have to rely on its own recruitment and training to face the future.

Above and below: Two of Israel's first North American P-51D Mustangs. The one in the upper photo is undergoing maintenance in the open. The one pictured below was soon to join 101 sqn as D-190. Later, when flown by American volunteer pilot, Wayne Peake, this aircraft shot down an RAF Mosquito PR 13 from 13 Sqn on a reconnaissance mission over Israel. Note the cartoon face on the fuselage *Magen David*, which was soon ordered to be removed, and the white/blue/white fuselage identification band.

Israeli Air Force
v
Royal Air Force

On 7 January 1949, during the final stages of 'Operation Chorev' which had the aim of evicting Egyptian Forces back over the international border dividing the Negev and Sinai, an event took place involving the IAF which could have resulted in serious ramifications for the new state of Israel.

Early in the morning, an Israeli military column was battling through fierce desert sandstorms near to the Egyptian border at Rafah, when it was spotted by a patrol of four Egyptian Spitfires who attacked them, raking the column with gunfire and destroying several vehicles which burst into flames and smoke. The column immediately broke into defensive fire positions and radioed for IAF assistance.

Responding to this call were two Spitfire Mk IXs of 101 Squadron piloted by Chalmers 'Slick' Goodlin and John McElroy who had been on patrol nearby, and quickly headed to where they spotted smoke rising from the burning vehicles in the distance. As they neared the Israeli position, they spotted three Spitfires apparently being chased off by ground fire and dived to attack. Opening fire as they closed, the Israeli aircraft shot all three out of the sky in quick succession.

However, these Spitfires were different from those that had attacked the column earlier. These were FR Mk 18s belonging to the Royal Air Force, and it was not the first time these two forces had clashed.

Defending Israeli air space
From the beginning of the conflict, the vapour trails of high flying reconnaissance aircraft had been seen over the skies of Israel. These had been identified as coming from the Mosquito PR 34s of 13 Squadron RAF, based at Fayid near the Suez Canal. With the close links between Great Britain and the Arabs, particularly Jordan and Egypt, the Israelis were concerned that the RAF was sharing the information obtained from these missions with the Arab forces. At first, Israel was powerless to stop these flights, however, the acquisition of the P-51D Mustangs gave them an aircraft with the speed and ceiling to make an interception.

On 20 November 1948, Wayne Peake, a 101 Squadron volunteer from the United States and former World War Two Mustang Pilot, entered the cockpit of Mustang D-190 at Hatzor Air Base, formerly RAF Kastina, and waited for the call to scramble. Further north at Ramat David, the Mosquito was spotted and the order given for Wayne to take off. Following its normal practice, the Mosquito PR 34, (VL625), circled the IAF Air Bases and headed out to sea.

Having the early warning, Wayne was ready waiting over Hatzor when the Mosquito arrived. To his colleagues on the ground who could see both aircraft, it seemed they would actually miss each other, but Wayne was above the Mosquito and at first could not see it beneath him. Putting his aircraft in a dive he spotted the intruder and soon caught up, but after firing several short bursts from his guns, they promptly jammed and the Mosquito flew on with no noticeable effect. However, Wayne's shooting had been on target and the Mosquito gradually lost height and was seen to be on fire, crashing into the sea without a trace. No more reconnaissance flights appeared over Israel.

Mistaken identity
The Royal Air Force Spitfire FR 18s shot down by McElroy and Goodlin were from a flight of four aircraft from 208 Squadron on a reconnaissance mission, checking that the Israeli Army was complying with the cease-fire and had withdrawn any units that had crossed into Sinai. One pair of aircraft flew low and the other pair high as they patrolled the border road between Auja and Rafah and it was over Rafah they were caught by the IAF.

As they approached the Israeli column near Rafah, the soldiers thought the Egyptians had returned for a further attack, and opened fire, hitting Spitfire TP387, whose pilot, Flight Sergeant Francis Close, was forced to bale out and become a prisoner of the Israelis. The three remaining Spitfires were breaking away from the ground fire when McElroy and Goodlin started their attack.

Canadian John McElroy was an experienced fighter pilot, having shot down ten *Luftwaffe* aircraft, and gaining a DFC and Bar during World War Two. He volunteered to join the IAF and had recently arrived on 101 Squadron, to wonder which of the three types of fighters it operated he was to fly. His wingman, Chalmers 'Slick' Goodlin, was also an experienced fighter pilot and a leading Test Pilot in the United States, having piloted the Bell X-1 in the quest for supersonic flight.

The RAF pilots had no idea of the presence of the Israeli aircraft and McElroy found himself on the tail of the trailing Spitfire TZ228, piloted by Flight Sergeant Ron Sayers. Firing as he overtook his target, McElroy's shells struck with devastating effect, killing Sayers and sending his Spitfire crashing below. He then lined up on Spitfire TP456 flown by Flying Officer Timothy McElhaw, and in a repeat, close range, performance sent this Spitfire crashing down. McElhaw managed to bale out

from his stricken aircraft.

As McElroy was chasing his second target, Goodlin was dog-fighting with the other remaining Spitfire, TP340 flown by Flying Officer Geoffrey Cooper, who, having been alerted to the Israeli aircraft after the shooting down of Sayers, began flying evasive manoeuvres denying Goodlin a clean shot. However, the Spitfire Mk IX is a more manoeuvrable machine than the Mk 18, and time was on Goodlin's side. He took the opportunity when it came, and his firing hit Cooper's engine forcing him to bale out. By this time the fight had drifted away from Rafah further into Sinai and Cooper was able to evade capture, and with the help of Bedouins, eventually make it back to his base. It was during this dog-fight that Goodlin recognised the roundels on the underside of Cooper's aircraft and realised that he and McElroy had just fought with the RAF.

During this action, no messages were sent by the RAF Spitfires to their base at Fayid and when the flight was overdue, fifteen Hawker Tempest Mk 6s from 6 and 213 Squadrons, and four more Spitfires from 208, were despatched to look for them. The Israelis, fearful of retaliation by the RAF, also mounted patrols over their column.

During the afternoon, a patrol of four IAF Spitfire Mk IXs led by Ezer Weizman, intercepted a flight of seven RAF Tempest VIs, mistaking their wing fuel tanks for bombs and thinking they were about the attack the IDF column. In the melée that followed, an IAF Spitfire flown by American volunteer William Schroeder, another World War Two veteran known as 'Sure-Shot', shot down Tempest NX207, killing the pilot, Pilot Officer David Tattersfield. Ezer Weizman also caught a Tempest in his gunsight observing hits, but having to break away as his own aircraft was hit in the tail by Tempest NX135 flown by Flight Lieutenant Brian Spragg of 6 Squadron. The Tempest hit by Ezer Weizman was NX134 flown by Flight Sergeant Douglas Liquorish, who managed to coax his damaged aircraft back to Deversoir in the Canal Zone.

When the Israelis broke off and returned to base, there were no celebrations and many heavy hearts. The visibility had been poor with sand and smoke in the air during the initial confrontation making identification difficult. The next day a telegram was sent to the RAF Headquarters in Cyprus, saying sorry, but pointing out that as a sovereign state Israel had a right to protect its airspace. The dead pilots were buried with Full Military Honours, whilst the prisoners were well treated and soon returned to the RAF in Cyprus.

P-51D Mustang, D-190, of 101 Sqn Hatzor, November 1948
This was the aircraft in which ex-USAAF World War Two Mustang pilot, American volunteer, Wayne Peake, shot down the RAF Mosquito PR.34, VL625 of 13 Sqn on 20 November 1948. The aircraft was natural metal finish overall with 'silver' painted laminar flow wings and fabric covered flying surfaces. Spinner was red and the rudder red and white diagonal stripes. Note the white/blue/white identification band around the rear fuselage.

Spitfire Mk IXe, 2021, '16' of 101 Sqn Hatzor, January 1949
Flown by Chalmers 'Slick' Goodlin, another American volunteer pilot, this was one of the aircraft involved in the engagement with 208 Sqn RAF Spitfires on 7 January 1949, and in which he shot down TP340, flown by F/O Geoffrey Cooper. The aircraft was still in its original Dark Green and Ocean Grey uppersurfaces with Medium Sea Grey undersides at this time. The numeral '16' was white, with the serial number 2021 in black under the tailplane. The spinner was red and the rudder red and white diagonal stripes.

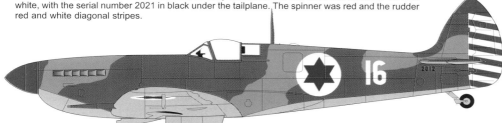

Spitfire FR.18, TZ233 'T' of 208 Sqn., Fayid, Palestine, early 1949
This Spitfire was on No 208 Squadron's strength at the same time as the four FR.18s that were shot down on the 7 January engagement. The aircraft is finished in Dark Green and Ocean Grey uppersurfaces with Medium Sea Grey undersides. Note the post-war red/white/blue roundels in the six positions, the white individual aircraft letter 'T' under the cockpit canopy and the red propeller spinner.

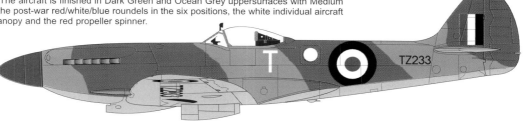

Tempest Mk VI, NX135, JV•V of 6 Sqn., Fayid, Palestine, early 1949
This Tempest was one of eight from 6 Sqn., (in company with another seven from 213 Sqn., and four more Spitfire FR.18s from 208 Sqn), that went to search for the four 'missing' 208 Sqn Spitfires on the afternoon of 7 January. By this period, No 6 Sqn had repainted most of its Tempests in Aluminium overall, with post-war red/white/blue roundels in the six positions. Note the roundel blue squadron code letters, the yellow spinner with black backplate and the official 6 Sqn badge, an eagle preying on a snake roughly forming a numeral 6.

Mosquito PR.34, VL625 'F' of 13 Sqn., Fayid, Palestine, late 1948
The photo reconnaissance Mosquito PR.34 that Wayne Peake shot down in his P-51D Mustang on 20 November 1948. No 13 Squadron's PR Mosquitoes were painted Aluminium overall, with post-war red/white/blue roundels in six positions. The individual aircraft letter 'F' is speculative.

© M.D.Howley 2000

Chapter 2

Trials of a Fledgling Air Force
Developing an Air Force

The War of Independence had left the Israeli armed forces in a perilous condition, with the State's resources drained and its economy undeveloped. The emphasis was on building the State and the Military budgets were tightened, which had a big effect on the Air Force.

The decade started with the air force striving for its existence as the Chief of Staff, seeing the Army as the prime service, sought to reduce the status of the Air Force to that of a Branch of the Army such as the Artillery. These arguments and lack of funding led to the resignation of Air Force Chief Ramez and his successor was appointed from the Army. Major General Shlomo Shamir had commanded a Brigade during the War of Independence and immediately prior to his Air Force appointment had been Head of the new Israeli Navy! He

was not to last long as ill health led to the appointment of Major General Chaim Laskov the following year. However, both were to make their mark on the Air Force.

At the end of the War of Independence, the IAF had received one hundred and twenty-one aircraft out of one hundred and forty-seven actually purchased. Of these one hundred and twenty-one, thirty-three had been lost through combat or accidents and forty-three others were grounded for various reasons, leaving only forty-five that were operational. Key amongst operational types were the No 101 Squadron Spitfires and Mustangs at Ramat David.

To replace the *Mahal* volunteers, a training school was established at Kfar Sirkin, opening on 1 January 1950, with

Heading: A line up of 101 Sqn Spitfire Mk IXes at Ramat David. In 1951, the squadron standardised on the P-51D Mustang, and all the Spitfires went to two other squadrons, in an Operational Training role. These were the 'Scorpion' Squadron with yellow and black rudder stripes, and the 'Lions Head' Squadron with blue and white rudder stripes.

Below: North American AT-6 Harvard, '06', of the Flying School, Tel Nof, mid-1950s. These aircraft were painted in the standard IAF Blue and Brown uppersurface colours and Light Grey undersides. Note the '06' numeral repeated on the fuselage and rudder with that on the fuselage appearing to be partially painted over. This aircraft also appears to have received recent alteration and the replacement of an engine cowling which does not seem to match the exhaust manifold position fitted to this sub-type of AT-6.

Above: As many of the foreign volunteers returned back to their home countries after the War of Independence, the IAF instituted a Flying Training School at Kfir Sirkin. Here Israeli pilots were taught on the Boeing Stearman Kaydet before moving on to the Spitfire.

North American Harvards and Boeing Stearman Kaydets for pilot training and with Airspeed Consuls and Avro Ansons for multi-engine and navigator training. Altogether fifteen Consuls were purchased and given serial numbers 2801 to 2815. The Ansons also mostly came from Great Britain with nine eventually entering the inventory and given numbers 2901 to 2909.

Tel-Nof was still busy as a transport base and as home for many of the other types in service. Light aircraft were still located on sites in the north and south of the country. The sheer diversity of aircraft types presented maintenance problems, although in some cases, such as the Beaufighters, the environment and combat missions had taken their toll, and

Above: Multi-engine Pilot Training and Navigation Training took place on the Airspeed Consul, the civil version of the military Airspeed Oxford. Fifteen were purchased and remained in service until 1956.

Below: Navigation Training was carried out on the Avro Anson. Nine had been purchased from Britain and South Africa but only a few made it to Israel at the end of the War of Independence. Four Ansons were detained by Greece after landing to refuel at Rhodes and were not returned to the Israelis until 1949.

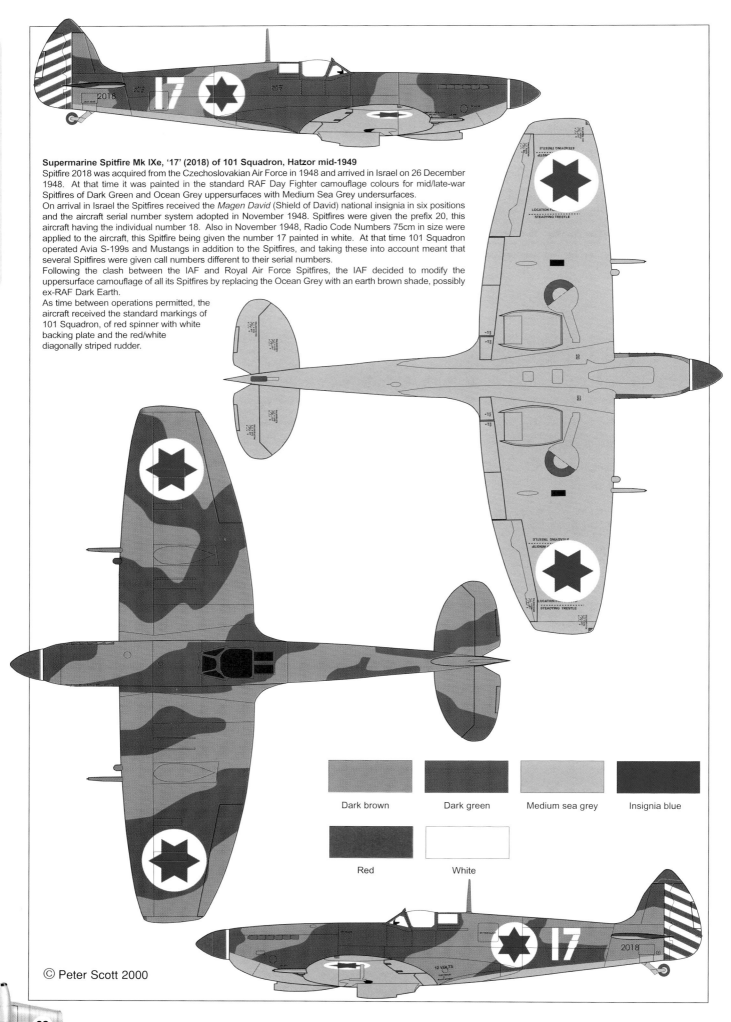

Supermarine Spitfire Mk IXe, '17' (2018) of 101 Squadron, Hatzor mid-1949

Spitfire 2018 was acquired from the Czechoslovakian Air Force in 1948 and arrived in Israel on 26 December 1948. At that time it was painted in the standard RAF Day Fighter camouflage colours for mid/late-war Spitfires of Dark Green and Ocean Grey uppersurfaces with Medium Sea Grey undersurfaces.

On arrival in Israel the Spitfires received the *Magen David* (Shield of David) national insignia in six positions and the aircraft serial number system adopted in November 1948. Spitfires were given the prefix 20, this aircraft having the individual number 18. Also in November 1948, Radio Code Numbers 75cm in size were applied to the aircraft, this Spitfire being given the number 17 painted in white. At that time 101 Squadron operated Avia S-199s and Mustangs in addition to the Spitfires, and taking these into account meant that several Spitfires were given call numbers different to their serial numbers.

Following the clash between the IAF and Royal Air Force Spitfires, the IAF decided to modify the uppersurface camouflage of all its Spitfires by replacing the Ocean Grey with an earth brown shade, possibly ex-RAF Dark Earth.

As time between operations permitted, the aircraft received the standard markings of 101 Squadron, of red spinner with white backing plate and the red/white diagonally striped rudder.

Dark brown   Dark green   Medium sea grey   Insignia blue

Red   White

© Peter Scott 2000

Spitfire Mk IXe, '15' (2008) of 101 Squadron January 1949
This aircraft was flown by Canadian national, John McElroy, who shot down two RAF Spitfire FR.18s of 208 Squadron on 7 January 1949. McElroy was a former RCAF World War Two pilot with ten *Luftwaffe* aircraft to his credit, and holder of the DFC and Bar. Camouflage scheme was the original delivery Dark Green and Ocean Grey uppersurfaces with Medium Sea Grey undersides.

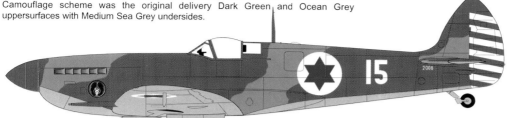

Spitfire Mk IXe, '31', 2015 of 101 Squadron, Hatzor, 1949
A repainted machine in Dark Green and 'earth brown' (possibly ex-RAF Dark Earth) uppersurfaces. The original Ocean Grey was overpainted, following the clash with similarly camouflaged RAF Spitfires. Standard 101 Squadron markings of red spinner and red/white striped rudder were applied, although the 'winged skull' squadron badge wasn't in this instance.

Spitfire IXc, '10', 2001, of 101 Squadron, Ramat David, 1949
This aircraft was one of the first Spitfires put together from spare parts and originally served as D-130. By late 1949, it had been stripped of all paintwork and was flown in overall natural metal with black anti-glare panel. Note that the 20mm cannon barrels have been removed indicating a non-operational role.

North American AT-6 Harvard '1105'
Harvards were acquired from the United States and six entered IAF service during the War of Independence where they served as ground attack aircraft. Harvard 1105 was one of these aircraft, flying as 'B-67'. After the war, with the need for pilot training, as most of the *Mahad* volunteers had returned home, the Harvards reverted to their traditional role as trainers. Uppersurfaces were green and brown, with yellow Training Bands painted on the fuselage and wings. The engine cowling and front section of the nose was also painted yellow.

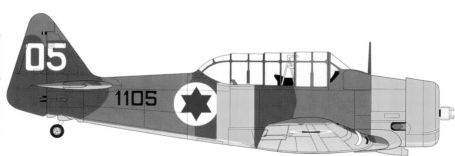

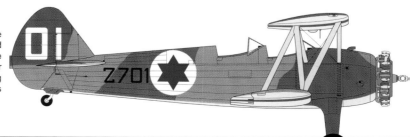

Boeing Stearman PT-17 Kaydet, 31, of Flying School, Kfir Sirtain, 1953
The Stearman was the favoured aircraft for training pilots and was preferred over its replacement, the Fokker S-11, which went to other roles in 1953. By this time the Stearmans were in silver dope with red Training Bands on wings and fuselage.

Boeing Stearman PT-17 Kaydet, 2701, circa 1950
Painted in the green/brown uppersurface camouflage with light grey undersides, red bands were painted under the wings signifying the training role. These aircraft were kept busy with the introduction of a major training programme to serve the needs of the growing IAF. On 1 January 1950 the Flying School was established on the former RAF airfield at Kfir Sirkin.

© M.D.Howley 2000

Above: Fokker S-11 05 restored at the IAF Museum. In 1957 the IAF acquired forty of this type for its pilot training, however it was not a success and in 1953 began to be transferred to the Light Aircraft Squadron and the IAF reverted back to Stearman Kaydets.

they had reached the end of their useful operational life. The IAF needed to concentrate on fewer aircraft types and operate them within its capabilities. Above all, it wanted to modernise to keep pace with other airforces, particularly those against which it may have to again fight.

Improving training

To improve the quality and availability of training aircraft, forty-one Fokker S.11 Instructors were purchased from the Netherlands. Painted overall Trainer

Below: DH Mosquito FB.6, K-2128, (Hebrew *Krav* = fighter) coming in to land at Hatzor Air Base. This Mosquito arrived from France in November 1951. Note the Catalina in the background. At this time these served with 69 Sqn which also operated the B-17s from Hatzor as part of Wing 4.

Yellow and given serial numbers 3101 to 3141, these side-by-side trainers were delivered by sea during 1951, but in the event, had a short career, being withdrawn in favour of the Stearmans in 1953, and after a spell in the light transport role, were sold on the civil market from 1954 onwards. Incidentally, the Fokkers were originally selected after a competition which involved the IAF also looking at the DH Chipmunk and the Temco T-35 Buckaroo.

1951 also saw the purchase of additional P-51D Mustangs from Sweden which gradually replaced the Spitfires in 101 Squadron. This purchase was part of a proposal by the head of the Air Force to bolster the front line aircraft which was also where he saw a priority. At the time of this purchase of second-hand aircraft for its Front Line squadron, the next fighter aircraft generation of F-86 Sabres and MiG-15s were battling over Korea.

The age of their aircraft did not affect the operational readiness of the Squadron however. In May 1950, four

Spitfires were scrambled to intercept an unidentified aircraft flying over northern Israel. The aircraft was identified as an RAF Short Sunderland Flying Boat on its way to Egypt, and was forced down to

Opposite page top: A line-up of Mosquito FB.6s of the 'Valley' Squadron, early 1953. These aircraft were painted with black rudders and spinners, but only K-2105 sports the Squadron badge, on the fin. In October 1953, whilst being flown by Lt Ovadya Nachman, K-2105 disintegrated in mid-air following an explosion of fumes in the left wing tank.

Opposite page middle: Another line-up, this time of 'Knights of the North' Mosquitoes at Hatzor on Independence Day, 25 April 1955. Mosquito FB.6, K-2135 arrived from France in November 1951 and remained in service until 1957. Note the red spinners and rudder usually associated with the 'Valley' Squadron.

Opposite page below: Two Mosquito FB.6s taxiing at Hatzor early 1950s. The leading Mosquito sports red spinners and rudder, but does not have the type's prefix number, 21, as part of its serial. K-11 arrived in Israel from France in July 1951, and sports red spinners and rudder.

Above: Mosquito PR.16 of the Photography Unit, (later to become the 'Flying Dragon' Sqn), based at Hatzor in the mid-1950s. This aircraft was one of four two-stage Merlin PR Mosquitoes acquired from France, all of which were finished in an overall painted Aluminium scheme with matt black anti-dazzle panel.

Right: Mosquito FB.6 of the 'Knights of the North' Sqn., undergoing maintenance on the Wing 4 maintenance centre at Hatzor. The way the aircraft has its tail lifted, and the access panels to the gun bays are removed, suggests work is being done on the 0.303 inch machine guns and 20mm cannons. Note the black spinners and the Squadron badge on the cockpit access door.

Below right: A flight of Mosquitoes over Northern Israel in the early 1950s. Mosquito FB.6, serialled 2103, was delivered from France in June 1951 and served until September 1955, when it was written-off after being involved in an accident.

land near Tel Aviv. The crew had no idea they had penetrated Israeli airspace and presented their maps as defence, as these did not show the new State of Israel. The RAF soon updated its maps after this incident.

By this time, the IAF Spitfires had been partially repainted when, following the clashes with the RAF, it was decided to overpaint the Ocean Grey with Dark Earth. This would help differentiate the camouflage colours between Israeli and RAF Spitfires, and produced a camouflage scheme more in keeping with the region's topography.

Two further Spitfire Squadrons were formed, and more Spitfires were acquired from Italy. The 'Scorpion' Squadron was identified by its Black and Yellow striped rudders and the 'Lions-Head' Squadron, with Blue and White rudders. However, these Spitfires would soon be relegated to the Operational Training role and many were eventually passed on to Burma. As the Spitfires became relegated to the role of Operational Trainers, they began to reappear in natural metal.

Enter the Mossie

In February 1951, the IAF signed a contract with France for the purchase of sixty-three DH Mosquitoes which were surplus to *Armée de l'Air* requirements. Most were in poor condition, languishing on storage sites at Chateaudun and Rennes. The contract covered four versions of the Mosquito; thirty-nine FB 6s, twenty NF 30s and four PR 16s. Later two further FB 6s and three T 3s were added, bringing the total to sixty-eight.

The contract also covered the supply of 20mm Hispano cannons and 0.303 inch Browning machine guns.

Work soon started on the refurbishment of the aircraft and from the numbers purchased, fifty-eight were brought up to flying condition. Delivery to Israel was contracted to the British company Britavia, which supplied Mosquito-experienced pilots for the job. All but one of the refurbished aircraft were delivered, as NF 30, 2156, crashed

Left opposite: Mosquito FB.6, K-2121 crash-landed at Hatzor 29 December 1953. This aircraft arrived from France in September 1951 and was allocated to the 'Knights of the North' Squadron. The crew members 2nd Lts Nachom Yaholom and Mordechai Segal survived the crash. Note the red spinners and rudder.

Left below : DH Mosquito PR.16, Z-2150, after a wheels-up belly landing at Hatzor on 1 October 1953. Z-2150, (*Zilum* = 'Photo Reconnaissance' in Hebrew), was delivered from France in May 1952. Note the black anti-dazzle panel in front of the windscreen and the B-17s in the background.

on its inspection flight killing IAF test pilot John Harvey. The Mosquitoes were allocated Israeli Air Force serial numbers starting with 2103, and apart from the T 3s which retained their overall Trainer Yellow colour scheme, and the NF 30s which were painted overall Black, all the FB 6s and PR 16s were painted silver.

With the introduction of the DH Mosquitoes, the IAF establised a unified command over all its multi-engined combat aircraft, and based all the Squadrons operating these types at Hatzor as 'Wing 4'. The Squadrons involved were:-
69 Squadron with Boeing B-17G Flying Fortresses
The 'Valley' Squadron with Mosquito FB 6s, Mosquito PR 16s and Mosquito T 3s. (Red spinners and rudder, Squadron Badge on Fin).
The 'Knights of the North' Squadron with Mosquito FB 6s and Mosquito NF 30s. (Black spinners and rudder, Squadron Badge on aircraft nose entry door).

Whilst at Hatzor, the Fortresses of 69 Squadron were joined by three Consolidated Catalina flying boats. Painted overall Dark Blue, these aircraft were given serials 3401 to 3403 and served as maritime patrol aircraft until being withdrawn in 1956.

Like other airforces at the time, the IAF decided to look at the potential of the helicopter to establish its usefulness to the service. During 1951, two Hiller 360s were acquired and given numbers 3301 and 3302.

Above: DH Mosquito FB.6, K-2109, of the 'Valley' Squadron at Hatzor armed with 5 inch HVAR rockets under its wings. This aircraft arrived from France in June 1951. Note the smaller blue *Magen David* star in the National Insignia, typical of those *Magen Davids* applied in France, and what appears to be quite a glossy black rudder.

Right: Arming a Mosquito FB.6 at Hatzor. The bombs appear to be American pattern 500lb bombs. Spinners are red, but there is no Squadron badge on the cockpit access door.

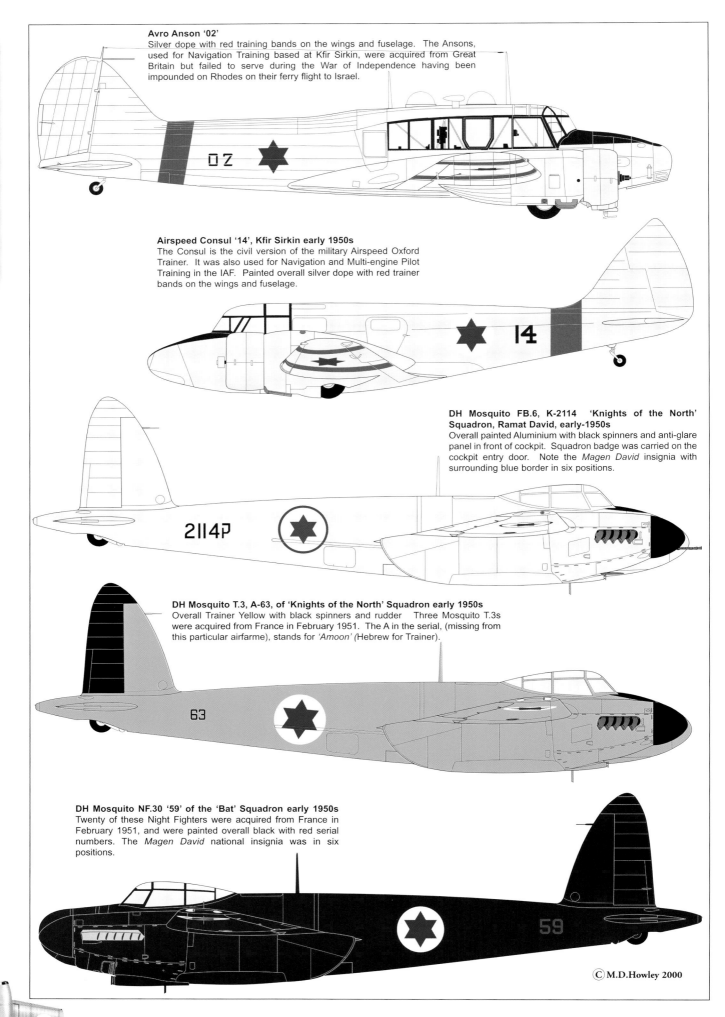

Avro Anson '02'
Silver dope with red training bands on the wings and fuselage. The Ansons, used for Navigation Training based at Kfir Sirkin, were acquired from Great Britain but failed to serve during the War of Independence having been impounded on Rhodes on their ferry flight to Israel.

Airspeed Consul '14', Kfir Sirkin early 1950s
The Consul is the civil version of the military Airspeed Oxford Trainer. It was also used for Navigation and Multi-engine Pilot Training in the IAF. Painted overall silver dope with red trainer bands on the wings and fuselage.

DH Mosquito FB.6, K-2114 'Knights of the North' Squadron, Ramat David, early-1950s
Overall painted Aluminium with black spinners and anti-glare panel in front of cockpit. Squadron badge was carried on the cockpit entry door. Note the *Magen David* insignia with surrounding blue border in six positions.

DH Mosquito T.3, A-63, of 'Knights of the North' Squadron early 1950s
Overall Trainer Yellow with black spinners and rudder   Three Mosquito T.3s were acquired from France in February 1951. The A in the serial, (missing from this particular airfarme), stands for *'Amoon'* (Hebrew for Trainer).

DH Mosquito NF.30 '59' of the 'Bat' Squadron early 1950s
Twenty of these Night Fighters were acquired from France in February 1951, and were painted overall black with red serial numbers. The *Magen David* national insignia was in six positions.

© M.D.Howley 2000

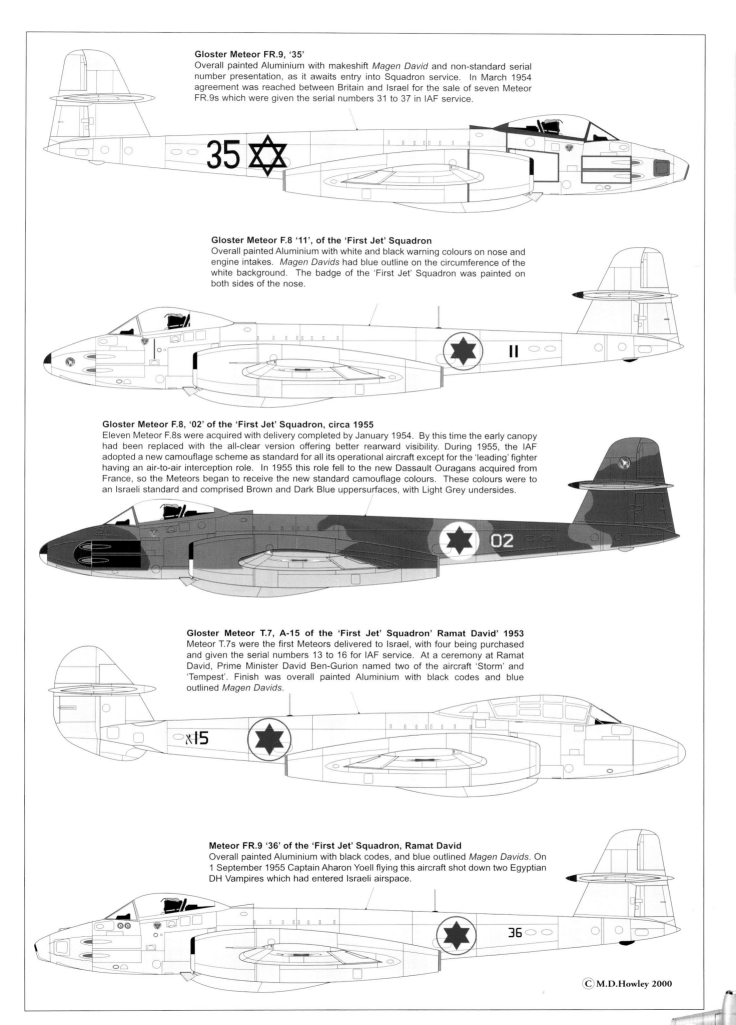

Gloster Meteor FR.9, '35'
Overall painted Aluminium with makeshift *Magen David* and non-standard serial number presentation, as it awaits entry into Squadron service. In March 1954 agreement was reached between Britain and Israel for the sale of seven Meteor FR.9s which were given the serial numbers 31 to 37 in IAF service.

Gloster Meteor F.8 '11', of the 'First Jet' Squadron
Overall painted Aluminium with white and black warning colours on nose and engine intakes. *Magen Davids* had blue outline on the circumference of the white background. The badge of the 'First Jet' Squadron was painted on both sides of the nose.

Gloster Meteor F.8, '02' of the 'First Jet' Squadron, circa 1955
Eleven Meteor F.8s were acquired with delivery completed by January 1954. By this time the early canopy had been replaced with the all-clear version offering better rearward visibility. During 1955, the IAF adopted a new camouflage scheme as standard for all its operational aircraft except for the 'leading' fighter having an air-to-air interception role. In 1955 this role fell to the new Dassault Ouragans acquired from France, so the Meteors began to receive the new standard camouflage colours. These colours were to an Israeli standard and comprised Brown and Dark Blue uppersurfaces, with Light Grey undersides.

Gloster Meteor T.7, A-15 of the 'First Jet' Squadron' Ramat David' 1953
Meteor T.7s were the first Meteors delivered to Israel, with four being purchased and given the serial numbers 13 to 16 for IAF service. At a ceremony at Ramat David, Prime Minister David Ben-Gurion named two of the aircraft 'Storm' and 'Tempest'. Finish was overall painted Aluminium with black codes and blue outlined *Magen Davids*.

Meteor FR.9 '36' of the 'First Jet' Squadron, Ramat David
Overall painted Aluminium with black codes, and blue outlined *Magen Davids*. On 1 September 1955 Captain Aharon Yoell flying this aircraft shot down two Egyptian DH Vampires which had entered Israeli airspace.

© M.D.Howley 2000

Left opposite: DH Mosquito FB.6 of the 'Knights of the North' Squadron at Hatzor in December 1953. The Squadron badge was located on the Mosquito's cockpit entry door on the right of the fuselage. The 'Bird on the Cloud' badge was designed by the Squadron Commander, Captain Hugo Marom, standing nearest to the engine. His successor as Squadron Commander, Captain Israel Lahav, stands next to him holding the entry ladder.

Left below: Mosquito T.3 Trainer, A-2125 (A = *Amoon*, Trainer in Hebrew), which came to grief during a training flight. Three Mosquito T.3s were acquired from France in February 1951, and retained their overall yellow colour schemes, with coloured rudders - either black or red, denoting attachment to either the 'Knights of the North' or the 'Valley' squadrons

engineering at London University. He was an experienced pilot and was referred to as a 'typical English Gentleman' from his time with the RAF, but he was a child of Tel Aviv. As Commander of the Air Force, he battled for what he believed to be right for Israel, and established a number of principles which were to influence the IAF for many years ahead. Basically, these principles were:-

•Israel could never afford to purchase specialised aircraft types, so must look for the best multi-role types it could afford.

•The IAF must maintain a high level of alert, ready to defend Israel around the clock and be the first to respond in a conflict emergency.

•The IAF must develop a qualitative advantage over any enemy, with high standards required for both air and ground crews. The IAF had one of the toughest flying courses in the world, with high washout rates for those who did not meet the standards required. (In June 1959 only one pilot graduated from Flying Course 30). Ground crews were not exempt as a programme of rapid

Below: Gloster Meteor T.7, '17', of the 'First Jet' Squadron, Ramat David late 1954. Overall painted Aluminium, with the national insignia in six positions. The black and white warning markings on engine intakes and nose were common to most IAF operated Meteors. Initially, four T.7s were delivered to the IAF in 1953, and this led to another order for two more in March 1954. These were numbered 17 and 18.

Further development

Both Shamir and Laskov started the process of developing a modern Air Force for Israel, in spite of the budget limitations, and always having to fight their corner within the IDF. They laid the foundations from which the Air Force could grow, starting a Flying School and a Technical School and integrating the Air Force into the IDF Command Structure. It was to emerge as an equal arm with the Army and Navy, under a Military High Command headed by the IDF Chief of Staff. The Air Force began to develop its own operating doctrine suiting its unique circumstances whilst also developing professional standards. Professionalism became synonymous with the next head of the Air Force, Colonel (later Major general) Dan Tolkovski who took office on 5 May 1953.

Air Force Commander Dan Tolkovski was a veteran of World War Two, having served in the RAF after studying

Right: North American P-51D Mustang, (i/d number uncertain), of the 'Flying Wing' Squadron, early 1956. In November 1955, 101 Squadron disbanded to prepare to become the first Mystère IVA squadron. Its Mustangs were transferred to the 'Scorpion' Squadron, which subsequently relinquished the long serving Spitfire, onto the newly formed 'Flying Wing' Squadron. By this time, Mustangs were camouflaged in Blue and Brown uppersurfaces, with Light Grey undersurfaces, although the paintwork was worn and flaking on many aircraft.

turnaround timing was introduced to get combat aircraft refuelled and re-armed as quickly as possible and back into the fight. Professionalism was the order of the day.

•A command and control system needed to be established to co-ordinate air defence and ground attack missions, particularly to communicate with other parts of the IDF. This would assist the IAF with its first priority of gaining air superiority, and the destruction of enemy air forces, particularly whilst they were still on the ground.

The IAF still had to argue for its budget, but Tolkovski could be as tough as his Army and Navy colleagues who were also striving for new equipment. The IAF received its first new equipment on 17 June 1953.

Israel Enters the Jet Age

After the years of trying to obtain modern jet aircraft had all come to nothing, suddenly in an effort to open up markets in the Middle East, the British Government offered to sell Gloster Meteor jet fighters to Israel. However, with typical British even-handedness of the time, this also applied to Iraq, Syria and Lebanon who were also offered the same deal. Egypt was already a jet operator having signed an agreement for Meteors and DH Vampires in 1950. Colonel Tolkovski came to Britain on 1 February 1953 and signed an agreement for eleven Meteor F 8s and four Meteor T 7s. Included in the agreement was conversion training for IAF pilots with the RAF.

The Meteor T 7s were delivered first, and given fictitious serial numbers (2162 - 2165), for the ferry flight, but were re-numbered 13 - 16 for IAF squadron service. The first two aircraft landed at Ramat David on 17 June 1953 to join the

Above middle: Two of the PBY-5A Catalinas, showing the application of *Magen David* national insignia on the nose, and serial numbers in white at the base of the fin. The Catalinas were given the serial numbers 3401, 3402 and 3403.

Above: Nearly not a photograph of a Catalina (!), but interesting none-the-less insofar as note the size and position of the underwing *Magen David* on the wing tip float fairing. The national insignia was carried in six positions.

Below: Consolidated PBY-5A Catalina on arrival in Israel from the United States and devoid of any national insignia and serial numbers. Three Catalinas were acquired, and were painted dark blue overall, and served as part of 69 Sqn on Maritime Patrol duties, with the B-17s in Wing 4 at Hatzor. They also operated on detachment from Haifa.

Consolidated PBY5A Catalina, '3401', early 1950s
Three Catalinas were acquired for the IAF and served from 1951 to 1956 in the maritime patrol role.
The Catalinas were painted Dark Blue overall and given the serial numbers 3401 to 3403.

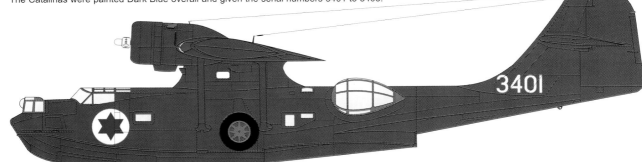

Fokker S-11 Instructor, '14', Kfir Sirkin, early 1950s
Forty S-11s were purchased for the IAF as the standard initial training aircraft. However, the type was not a success and they were transferred to the Light Aircraft Squadron from 1953 onwards. They were painted overall Trainer Yellow with red rudders.

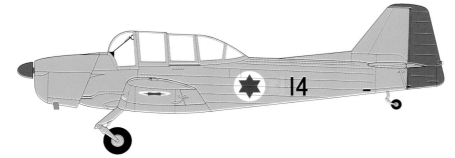

Hiller 360 Helicopter '02', attached to the Flying School at Kfir Sirkin 1951
This Hiller 360, used to evaluate the helicopter for use in the IAF, was finished in overall Trainer Yellow, with black serial number 02 and national insignia on the underside behind nose wheel. Rotor blades were painted black.

Dassault MD 450 Ouragan '43' of the 'Hornet' Squadron in 1955
The Ouragan was acquired as the IAF waited for delivery of the Mystere IVA fighter from France. The Hornet Squadron was chosen to lead the type into IAF service. They were in natural metal, but soon sported a large *sharkmouth* nose and lightning flash on the wing-tip tanks.

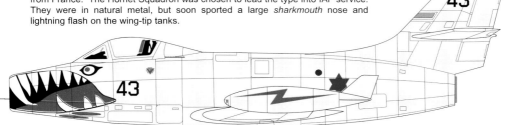

DH Chipmunk 3001, Flying School 1950.
The Chipmunk was evaluated as a potential training aircraft for the IAF, but its poor performance meant it lost out to the Fokker S-11 Instructor. Finish was painted Aluminium overall, with black anti-glare panel and spinner.

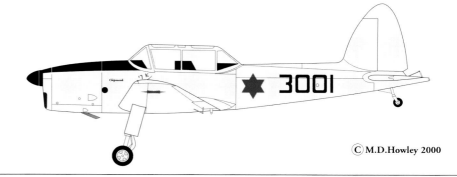

© M.D.Howley 2000

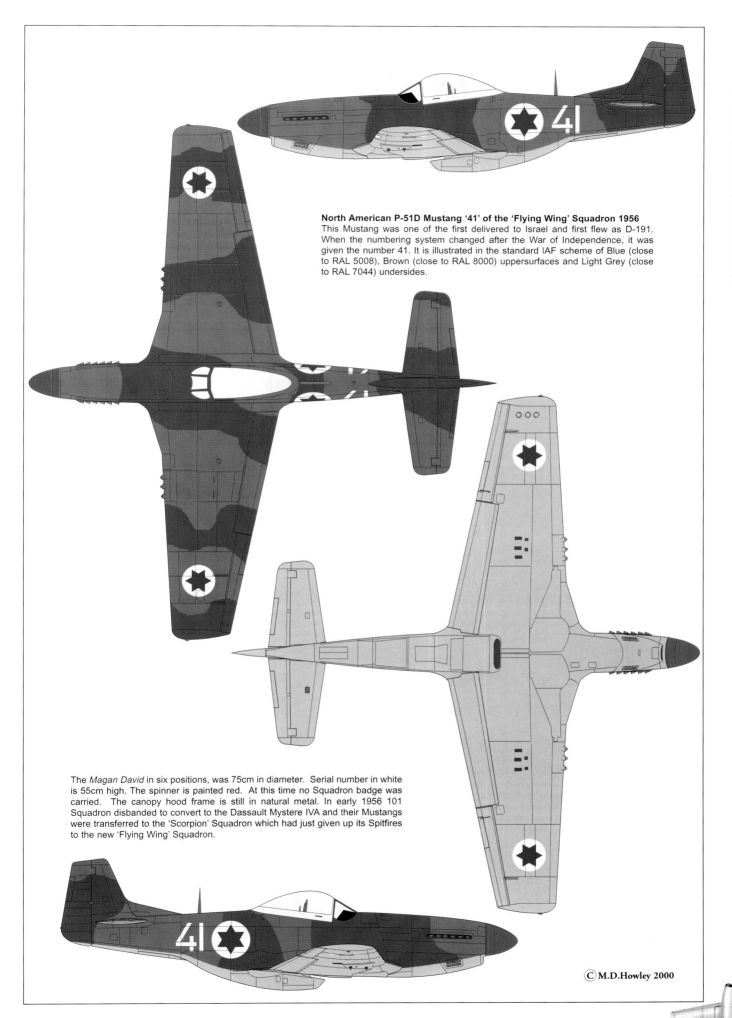

North American P-51D Mustang '41' of the 'Flying Wing' Squadron 1956
This Mustang was one of the first delivered to Israel and first flew as D-191. When the numbering system changed after the War of Independence, it was given the number 41. It is illustrated in the standard IAF scheme of Blue (close to RAL 5008), Brown (close to RAL 8000) uppersurfaces and Light Grey (close to RAL 7044) undersides.

The *Magan David* in six positions, was 75cm in diameter. Serial number in white is 55cm high. The spinner is painted red. At this time no Squadron badge was carried. The canopy hood frame is still in natural metal. In early 1956 101 Squadron disbanded to convert to the Dassault Mystere IVA and their Mustangs were transferred to the 'Scorpion' Squadron which had just given up its Spitfires to the new 'Flying Wing' Squadron.

© M.D.Howley 2000

Above: Sharing Hatzor air base with the Mosquito FB,6s in Wing 4, were the Boeing B-17s of 69 Squadron. By this time, the B-17s had been restored with their full armament suite of turrets. This particular machine, 1602, (the number erased by the Israeli censor), was also equipped with AN/APS 4 nose-mounted search radar in the Maritime Reconnaissance role. Note the nose art, (an eagle?), on the forward fuselage.

'First Jet' Squadron formed just ten days earlier. On 23 June 1953, Prime Minister David Ben Gurion visited the new squadron and at the ceremony named the two aircraft 'Suefa' (Storm) and 'Sa'ar' (Tempest) from the verse in Psalm 83: "Thus you shall chase them in your tempest and in your storm frighten them". Delivery of the Meteor F 8s soon followed and was completed by January 1954. Unlike RAF Meteor Mk 8s, these aircraft were equipped to carry eight 5 inch HVAR Rockets under their wings.

However, eleven Meteors were not adequate for the IAF needs, and in March 1954 agreement was reached for the sale of nine more aircraft comprising seven Meteor FR 9s and two further T 7s. Delivery of these was completed by May 1955. The Meteor FR 9s were given ferry numbers 211 to 217, but numbered 31 - 37 in squadron service. The Meteor T 7s had ferry numbers 111 and 112, but numbered 17 to 18 in IAF squadron service. Unlike the previous delivery, which were new build aircraft, all these Meteors had previously served with the RAF.

The 'First Jet' Squadron worked hard to achieve operational readiness, but when an incident occurred on 1 March 1954, it was other aircraft types that saved the day. The Israeli Patrol Boat *Almogit* ran aground off the Saudi Arabian coast and sent off a distress call for immediate assistance. A Dakota and several Mosquitoes were sent to the

Right: In 1951, the IAF purchased two Hiller 360 helicopters to evaluate the usefulness of helicopters for the service. They were given numbers 01 and 02.

scene. It had been decided that the *Almogit* should be abandoned, and covered by the circling Mosquitoes, seven Piper Cubs flew out from Eilat and landed on the beach near the stricken vessel, rescuing its crew. The ship was then destroyed by cannon and rocket fire by 101 Sqn Mustangs.

On 29 August 1955, the first jet combat in the Middle East occurred when two IAF Meteors intercepted four Egyptian Vampires that had crossed into Israeli air space in the south of the country. The Vampires were chased back to their own territory, with one of them claimed as 'damaged' by the IAF Meteors. Soon after, on 1 September, two IAF Meteors were scrambled to intercept other Egyptian Vampires seen crossing over the border. Flying the Meteors, Captains Aharon Yoeli and Yoash Tsidon soon spotted two Vampires and turned to attack, positioning themselves on the tails of the Egyptian aircraft. Captain Yoeli, flying Meteor FR 9 '36' shot down one Vampire and then turned on to his

alerted wingman who was manoeuvring into the Israelis. After a short series of twists and turns, Captain Yoeli shot that Vampire down too. Both EAF Vampires (1567 and 1569) were confirmed as they crashed well inside the Israeli border. Egyptian incursion flights stopped after this incident.

In 1955, the IAF did produce standard camouflage patterns for individual aircraft and standard colours. This was a Dark Blue and Medium Brown upper surface scheme with Light Grey Undersides. In addition to operating over land, the IAF also operated over the sea and developed a camouflage scheme to cope with both environments. The resulting colours are to an Israeli paint standard. There are no direct RAL/BS/FS equivalents, although FS 30215 Brown, RAL 5008 Blue and RAL 7044 Grey come close. Although a standard camouflage pattern did emerge appropriate to each aircraft type, it was not long before aircraft were spotted with reversed colours and even 'mirror' image patterns.

The French Period

Israel had developed a friendly relationship with the French Government as had been seen with the sale of the Mosquitoes and other military arms. In 1955 the Israelis were seeking a modern fighter to combat the MiGs that had been sold to Egypt. Interest was expressed in the F-86 Sabre, which the Canadian Government were seemingly willing to sell, and with the Dassault Mystère IIC which was offered by the French. The Sabre deal for twenty-four aircraft fell through when Canada joined others in an embargo on the supply of arms to the Middle East.

The French did not support this embargo, but the Israelis, unhappy about the performance of the Mystère IIC, reached a separate agreement for the sale of the more capable Dassault Mystère IV. As deliveries would take longer, the IAF placed an immediate order for the Dassault Ouragan which would act as a stop-gap measure. This decision proved right for the IAF, for in the Ouragan, they found an excellent, stable ground attack aircraft, eventually ordering seventy-five, whilst the Mystère IV proved more than capable of taking on the MiGs and over sixty entered service with the IAF.

When the Meteors, Ouragans, and Mystères, were first received, they operated in their natural metal finish state, and only gradually did they receive camouflage paint. It has been reported that the IAF had a policy of keeping its newest aircraft in natural metal, only painting them when other, later delivery types superseded them in their role. Whilst this was generally the case, to paint an aircraft meant taking it out of service, and had a material cost involved. Consequently the 'superseded' aircraft would only be painted as and when the time came for a major maintenance overhaul which justified both the 'down time' and the additional cost.

In addition to fighter aircraft, Israel also purchased eight Nord 2501 Noratlas twin engined transport aircraft. In natural metal with white fuselage tops, these aircraft would soon sport the Blue and Brown camouflage scheme. Allocated to the newly formed 'Flying Elephant' Squadron at Tel Nof, the Nord soon became a favourite for the transport and parachute roles. All these new aircraft types were to prove their worth in 1956.

Above: Nord 2501 Noratlas, 4X-FAU. In 1955 the IAF purchased eight Nords for use in the Transport and Paratroop roles by the 'Elephant' Squadron

Below: Dassault 450 Ouragan, with civil registration 4X-FRH at Hatzor in October 1955. The first Ouragans were to equip the newly formed 'Hornet' Squadron. Note the delivery number 5648.

Bottom: One of the first twelve Dassault Mystère IVAs at Hatzor in April 1956. 101 Sqn had been re-formed to operate the type. Note the delivery number 6646.

Chapter 3

The Sinai Campaign
'Operation Kadesh' and Suez

Following the War of Independence, an uneasy cease-fire existed between Israel and her neighbours, who still refused to recognise the new State. A pattern of terrorism emerged with Arab Commando Teams, the *Fedayeen* crossing the borders from Syria, Jordan and more especially, Egypt to cause murder and mayhem in the Jewish Settlements. Israel retaliated against these raids, mostly with ground troops, but occasionally, clashes led to the IAF becoming involved when they escalated to major incidents such as the shooting down of the Vampires as mentioned Chapter Two.

In 1955, President Nasser of Egypt entered a massive arms deal with Czechoslovakia for the supply of upto date Soviet equipment, which gave Egypt a massive military advantage over Israel. Over one hundred and twenty MiG-15 fighters, fifty Il-28 'Beagle' bombers and twenty Il-14 'Crate' transport aircraft were

included for the Egyptian Air Force.

Egypt had closed the Suez Canal to Israeli shipping and then closed the Straits of Tiran, blocking Israeli shipping from entering the Gulf of Aqaba and the Port of Eilat. But it was the Egyptian act of nationalising the Suez Canal, threatening British and French strategic interests, that precipitated the Suez War. Israel joined in an alliance with Britain and France who had decided to take military action against Egypt. For Israel, military action was important for three reasons:-
•To remove the threat of attack by Egypt on her southern borders
•To destroy the ability of the *Fedayeen* to make attacks on Israel
•To open the supply routes blockaded by Egypt.

With war imminent, the IAF began its preparations. Deliveries of the aircraft it had purchased from France were going as planned, with the Ouragan

establishing its usefulness on 12 April 1956, by shooting down an Egyptian Vampire. The IAF had also received further aircraft including another seven

Heading: Lt Colonels Ariel 'Arik' Sharon, (sitting with his back to the camera), and Rehavam 'Ghandi' Zeevi, pause for consultations at the Mitla Pass, which was assaulted by 400 IDF paratroopers on the night of 29 October 1956. The Piper Cubs of the 'Light Aircraft' Squadron flew many liaison and evacuation missions to Mitla, and one was severely damaged by fire following an attack by several Egyptian MiG-15s on the landing strip.

Below: A Dassault Ouragan 45 of the 'Hornet' Squadron during 'Operation Kadesh' in October 1956. The Ouragan was the first of the French jet aircraft purchased by the IAF, starting what was called their 'French' period. The Ouragan, armed with HVAR rockets and four 20mm cannons, proved itself to be a stable weapons platform and a capable ground-attack aircraft. Note the black and yellow identification bands on the wings and rear fuselage.

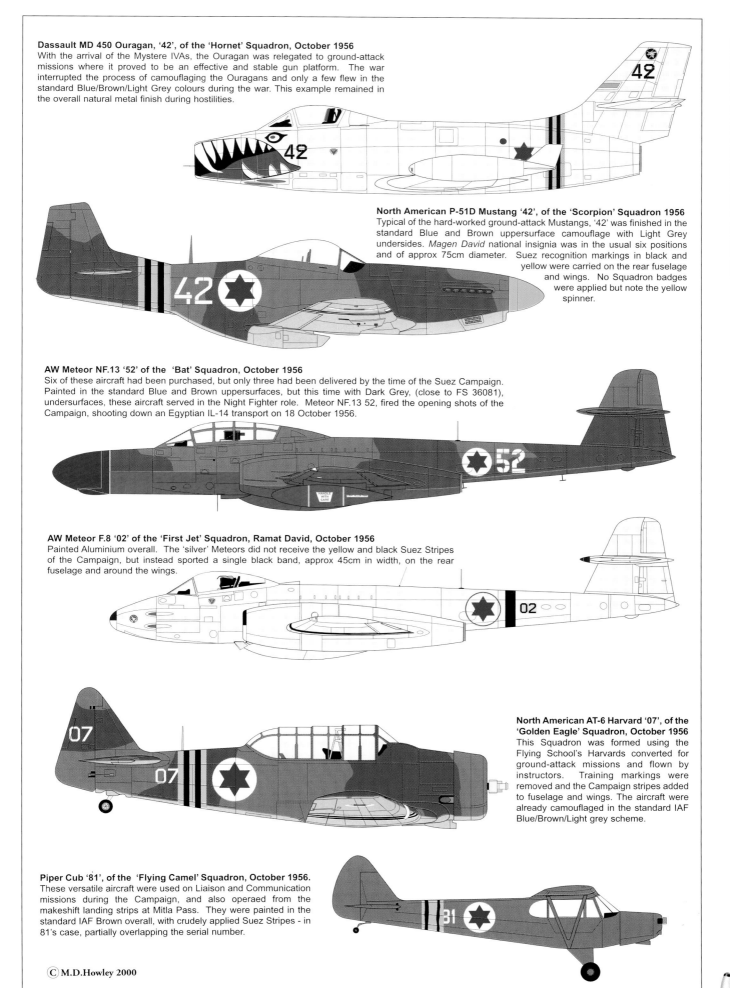

Dassault MD 450 Ouragan, '42', of the 'Hornet' Squadron, October 1956
With the arrival of the Mystere IVAs, the Ouragan was relegated to ground-attack missions where it proved to be an effective and stable gun platform. The war interrupted the process of camouflaging the Ouragans and only a few flew in the standard Blue/Brown/Light Grey colours during the war. This example remained in the overall natural metal finish during hostilities.

North American P-51D Mustang '42', of the 'Scorpion' Squadron 1956
Typical of the hard-worked ground-attack Mustangs, '42' was finished in the standard Blue and Brown uppersurface camouflage with Light Grey undersides. *Magen David* national insignia was in the usual six positions and of approx 75cm diameter. Suez recognition markings in black and yellow were carried on the rear fuselage and wings. No Squadron badges were applied but note the yellow spinner.

AW Meteor NF.13 '52' of the 'Bat' Squadron, October 1956
Six of these aircraft had been purchased, but only three had been delivered by the time of the Suez Campaign. Painted in the standard Blue and Brown uppersurfaces, but this time with Dark Grey, (close to FS 36081), undersurfaces, these aircraft served in the Night Fighter role. Meteor NF.13 52, fired the opening shots of the Campaign, shooting down an Egyptian IL-14 transport on 18 October 1956.

AW Meteor F.8 '02' of the 'First Jet' Squadron, Ramat David, October 1956
Painted Aluminium overall. The 'silver' Meteors did not receive the yellow and black Suez Stripes of the Campaign, but instead sported a single black band, approx 45cm in width, on the rear fuselage and around the wings.

North American AT-6 Harvard '07', of the 'Golden Eagle' Squadron, October 1956
This Squadron was formed using the Flying School's Harvards converted for ground-attack missions and flown by instructors. Training markings were removed and the Campaign stripes added to fuselage and wings. The aircraft were already camouflaged in the standard IAF Blue/Brown/Light grey scheme.

Piper Cub '81', of the 'Flying Camel' Squadron, October 1956.
These versatile aircraft were used on Liaison and Communication missions during the Campaign, and also operaed from the makeshift landing strips at Mitla Pass. They were painted in the standard IAF Brown overall, with crudely applied Suez Stripes - in 81's case, partially overlapping the serial number.

© M.D.Howley 2000

Right: Once in Israel, the Mosquito TR.33s, (a Naval version of the Mosquito with 4-blade propellers), served with the 'Knights of the North' Squadron at Hatzor and were the most popular Mosquitoes in the IAF to fly. During the Suez Campaign in 1956, the Squadron was based at Ramat David and participated in many missions over Sinai. Note the bomb racks and rocket rails under the wings, and lack of nose armament, plus *Magen David* national markings on the extreme underwing tips.

Below: DH Mosquito TR.33 at Blackbushe with the fictitious serial number 4x3186. In 1954 a contract was signed with British scrap dealer Mr R (Bob) Short for thirteen Mosquito TR.33s and seven Mosquito FB.6s. These were refurbished and ferried to Israel between November 1954 and August 1955.

DH Mosquito FB 6s and thirteen Mosquito TR 33s from Mr R (Bob) Short, a British Scrap Dealer. Later in 1956 came three Meteor NF 13s from a batch of six ordered two years previously. It was one of these aircraft that fired the first Israeli shots of the 1956 campaign.

Order of Battle

At the beginning of the Sinai Campaign, the IAF comprised:-

• The 'Hammers' Squadron with B-17G Flying Fortress bombers brought out of retirement and painted in the now standard Blue/Brown camouflage scheme.
• The 'Scorpions' Squadron with P-51D Mustangs, having given up its Spitfires earlier in the year. In standard Blue/Brown camouflage, the aircraft sported yellow spinners, but not the black/yellow stripped rudders as found on the Spitfires. The Mustangs did not carry any Squadron badges.

• The 'Flying Wing' Squadron with P-51D Mustangs, again in the standard Blue/Brown camouflage scheme, this time with red spinners and again no Squadron badges.
• The 'Knights of the North' Squadron with Mosquito FB 6s and TR 33s, in Blue/Brown standard camouflage colours, and no Squadron badges.
• The 'Flying Dragon' Squadron with Mosquito PR 16s in standard Blue/Brown camouflage colours, and no Squadron badges.
• The 'First Jet' Squadron with Meteor F 8s, FR 9s and T 7s. With the arrival of the Ouragan and Mystère, the Meteors had been 'relegated' to the ground-attack role and were beginning to be camouflaged in the standard Blue/Brown colours. At the time of Operation 'Kadesh', the Meteors went into action, some painted and some still in natural metal. No Squadron badges were carried on the painted examples.

• The 'Bats' Squadron with Meteor NF 13s, in the night fighter role, were painted in the standard Blue/Brown upper surface camouflage colours but with Dark Grey undersides. This colour, like the Blue and Brown top colours, was to an Israeli specification and was similar to Grey FS 36081. The Squadron badge was carried on the right fuselage side, below front of cockpit canopy.
• The 'Hornet' Squadron with MD Ouragans, again were in the process of being painted in the standard Blue/Brown camouflage colours, so during the Campaign appeared in camouflage and in natural metal. The distinctive *Sharkmouth* was painted on the aircraft after the Sinai Campaign, and no Squadron badges were carried.
• 101 Squadron was equipped with MD Mystère IV aircraft, in natural metal, and carried the Squadron badge on fin.
• The 'Golden Eagle' Squadron with NA Harvards from the Flying School, were equipped for ground-attack duties. Aircraft were painted in the standard Blue/Brown camouflage colours with no Squadron markings. The Yellow bands denoting training aircraft were removed for the Campaign.
• The 'Flying Camel' Squadron, largely equipped with Piper Cubs, were painted overall just in the standard camouflage Brown.
• The 'Flying Elephant' Squadron, were equipped with Transport aircraft. To assist IAF C-47 Dakotas and the few Nord Noratlas transports, other aircraft were requisitioned from *El Al* and *Arkia* Commercial Airlines. The IAF Dakotas were in a mix of standard Blue/Brown camouflage colours and natural metal. Noratlas transports were natural metal with a white fuselage top. The requisitioned commercial service aircraft

Left: AW Meteor NF.13, '57', of the 'Bat' Squadron. In 1956 the Squadron inherited the 'Bat on a Cloud' badge from the 'Knights of the North' and displayed this badge on the right front fuselage, so it would be in the same position as it had been on the Mosquito's cockpit entry door. The Squadron also added a red chevron outlined in white on the tail, which can be seen above the tailplane on the fin. A red chevron still appears on the tails of the 'Bat' Squadron aircraft today.

retained their normal civil markings.

•Other aircraft types in service, participating in the Campaign included two Sikorsky S-55 Helicopters, '02' and '03', in standard Blue/Brown camouflage colours.

•IAF aircraft not directly participating in the Sinai Campaign included, other Flying School aircraft, such as Harvards and Stearmans painted in overall Yellow and the Consuls and Ansons painted Silver, with red trainer markings on wings and fuselage.

Preparation

Following agreement with Britain and France, Israel would attack Egypt on 29 October 1956, with British and French Forces landing soon afterwards, ('Operation Musketeer') to retake the Suez Canal. To enable the Israelis to complete their part and to provide additional air defence in case of attack from Egypt, France stationed two Squadrons of Mystère IVs, (given fictitious IAF Squadron Numbers of 199 and 201 Squadrons) in Israel. Later a Squadron of F-84F Thunderstreaks, (given the fictitious IAF No 200 Squadron), was station at Lod in support of 'Operation Musketeer's attack on Egyptian airfields. Additional Nord Noratlas and ten Dakota transport aircraft were also supplied by France and painted in IAF colours and insignia.

All aircraft participating in the Campaign, Israeli French and British, were to be painted with Yellow and Black recognition stripes. For the IAF, these stripes were applied by brush, usually in a crude manner, with the black stripes positioned evenly in the yellow band or at the edges of the yellow bands. It differed from unit to unit or even aircraft within the same squadron. Bare metal Meteors flew with either just a black band around the rear fuselage, (eg aircraft 04), or around both the fuselage and the wings, (eg aircraft 02 and 06). Even requisitioned Commercial aircraft were painted with these recognition stripes.

Opening Shots

During the afternoon of 28 October 1956, it was learned that a delegation of the Egyptian Military High Command, led by Marshal Abdal Hakhim Amar, were in Damascus signing a Pact with Syria and Jordan and would be returning to Cairo in

their Ilyushin Il-14 'Crate' Transport that night. In an attempt to create confusion and command problems for the Egyptians, arrangements were made to intercept this aircraft.

The 'Bat' Squadron at that time had only received three of the six Meteor NF 13s that had been ordered, and only two were serviceable for action. These had been ordered specifically for night operations and were the first credible aircraft Israel possessed for that role, because the Mosquito NF 30s had been delivered without radar. Later a few NF 30s were equipped with the American AN/APS4 radar, but this proved unsuccessful.

Flying over the Mediterranean Sea between Israel and Cyprus, Captain Yoash 'Chatto' Tsiddon, with navigator Lieutenant Elyashiv 'Shivi' Brosh, in Meteor NF 13 '52' spotted the Il-14 and slowed down to attack. Closing at slow speed Tsiddon, opened fire, to discover that only the two port 20mm cannons were working. However, his first shots had hit the target but it continued on course. Tsiddon turned for a second attack, this time setting the Il-14's right wing on fire and causing it to crash into the sea. All aboard were killed, although Marshal Amar had decided to stay over in Syria and was not amongst the High Command passengers.

Before the full Operation was launched, there was one other important task to accomplish, the severing of the Egyptian communication links in Sinai. This mission had been allocated to the NA P-51D Mustangs of the 'Flying Wing' Squadron at Tel-Nof. Six Mustangs took off on the afternoon of 29 October 1956 and headed for western Sinai and the Bitter lakes. Trials had been undertaken, to bring down telegraph lines using a cable suspended from the Mustangs which severed the lines as the P-51s passed over them. This met with only moderate success and on the day, the telegraph lines were actually severed using the Mustangs' propellers and wingtips! Although needing some skillful low flying, the mission was successful and all the Mustangs returned safely.

Whilst the Mustangs were returning home, the IDF Assault Force tasked with capturing and holding the strategically important Mitla Pass, was en-route to their objective. Sixteen Dakotas loaded with the 400 men and equipment of the 890th Paratroop Battalion crossed into Sinai and headed for the Pass, with the assault drop planned for 17.00 hours. Escorting the Dakotas were Meteors and Ouragans, flying close support, whilst three quartets of Mystères mounted Combat Air Patrols over the drop zone

Two rather blurred, but none-the-less historic photographs of two of the first IAF Meteor NF.13s to see action.
Above: Underside view of an AW Meteor NF.13. In 1956, the IAF purchased six NF.13s of which three were delivered in time for action during the Suez Campaign. They were painted in the IAF standard camouflage colours of Brown and Dark Blue with Dark Grey undersides, befitting their night-fighter role.

Left: Armstrong Whitworth Meteor NF.13, '52', of the 'Bat' Squadron over Northern Israel. On the night of 28 October 1956, this aircraft fired the opening shots of the Suez Campaign by shooting down an Egyptian Air Force Il-14 transport, believed to be carrying members of the Egyptian Military High Command.

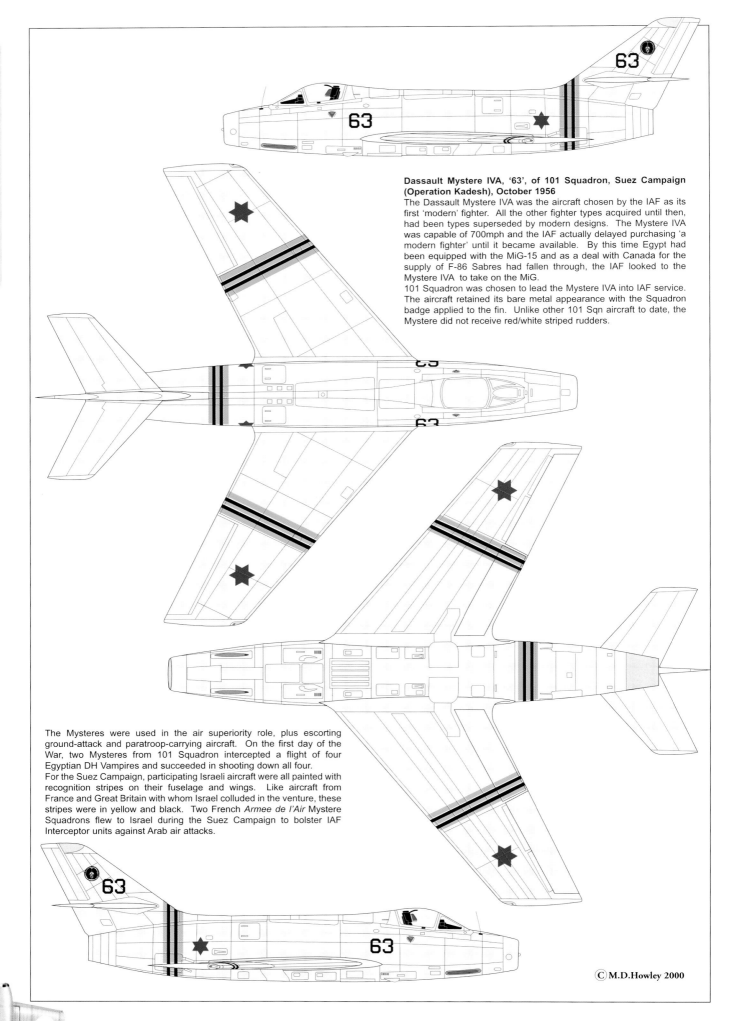

Dassault Mystere IVA, '63', of 101 Squadron, Suez Campaign (Operation Kadesh), October 1956

The Dassault Mystere IVA was the aircraft chosen by the IAF as its first 'modern' fighter. All the other fighter types acquired until then, had been types superseded by modern designs. The Mystere IVA was capable of 700mph and the IAF actually delayed purchasing 'a modern fighter' until it became available. By this time Egypt had been equipped with the MiG-15 and as a deal with Canada for the supply of F-86 Sabres had fallen through, the IAF looked to the Mystere IVA to take on the MiG.

101 Squadron was chosen to lead the Mystere IVA into IAF service. The aircraft retained its bare metal appearance with the Squadron badge applied to the fin. Unlike other 101 Sqn aircraft to date, the Mystere did not receive red/white striped rudders.

The Mysteres were used in the air superiority role, plus escorting ground-attack and paratroop-carrying aircraft. On the first day of the War, two Mysteres from 101 Squadron intercepted a flight of four Egyptian DH Vampires and succeeded in shooting down all four.

For the Suez Campaign, participating Israeli aircraft were all painted with recognition stripes on their fuselage and wings. Like aircraft from France and Great Britain with whom Israel colluded in the venture, these stripes were in yellow and black. Two French *Armee de l'Air* Mystere Squadrons flew to Israel during the Suez Campaign to bolster IAF Interceptor units against Arab air attacks.

© M.D.Howley 2000

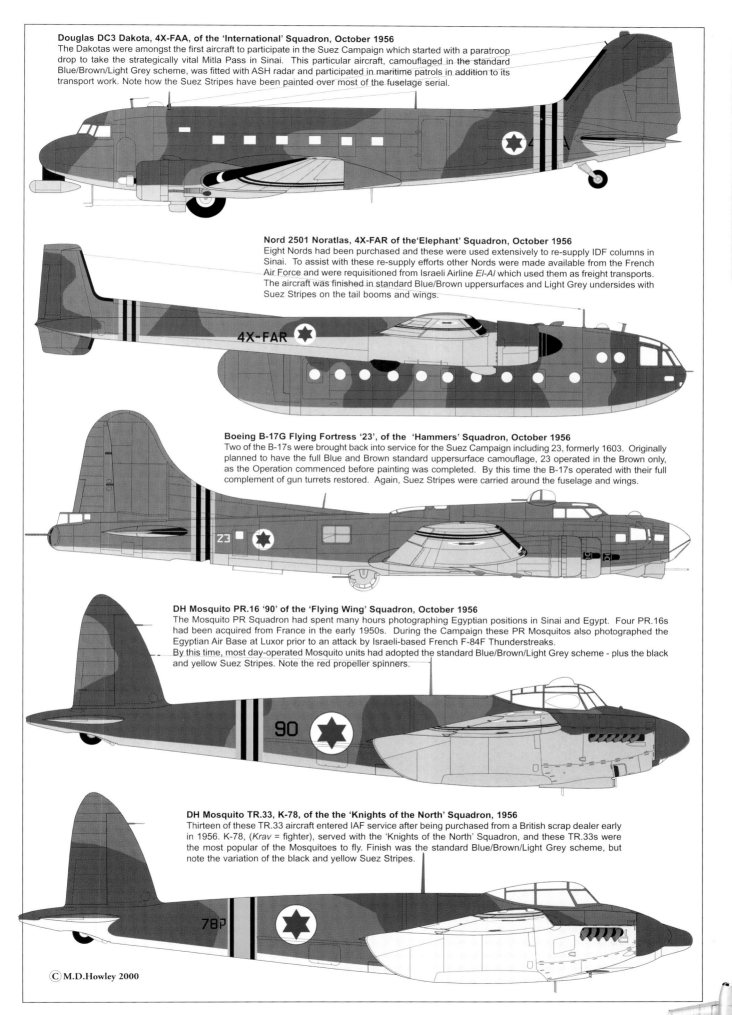

Douglas DC3 Dakota, 4X-FAA, of the 'International' Squadron, October 1956
The Dakotas were amongst the first aircraft to participate in the Suez Campaign which started with a paratroop drop to take the strategically vital Mitla Pass in Sinai. This particular aircraft, camouflaged in the standard Blue/Brown/Light Grey scheme, was fitted with ASH radar and participated in maritime patrols in addition to its transport work. Note how the Suez Stripes have been painted over most of the fuselage serial.

Nord 2501 Noratlas, 4X-FAR of the 'Elephant' Squadron, October 1956
Eight Nords had been purchased and these were used extensively to re-supply IDF columns in Sinai. To assist with these re-supply efforts other Nords were made available from the French Air Force and were requisitioned from Israeli Airline *El-Al* which used them as freight transports. The aircraft was finished in standard Blue/Brown uppersurfaces and Light Grey undersides with Suez Stripes on the tail booms and wings.

Boeing B-17G Flying Fortress '23', of the 'Hammers' Squadron, October 1956
Two of the B-17s were brought back into service for the Suez Campaign including 23, formerly 1603. Originally planned to have the full Blue and Brown standard uppersurface camouflage, 23 operated in the Brown only, as the Operation commenced before painting was completed. By this time the B-17s operated with their full complement of gun turrets restored. Again, Suez Stripes were carried around the fuselage and wings.

DH Mosquito PR.16 '90' of the 'Flying Wing' Squadron, October 1956
The Mosquito PR Squadron had spent many hours photographing Egyptian positions in Sinai and Egypt. Four PR.16s had been acquired from France in the early 1950s. During the Campaign these PR Mosquitos also photographed the Egyptian Air Base at Luxor prior to an attack by Israeli-based French F-84F Thunderstreaks.
By this time, most day-operated Mosquito units had adopted the standard Blue/Brown/Light Grey scheme - plus the black and yellow Suez Stripes. Note the red propeller spinners.

DH Mosquito TR.33, K-78, of the the 'Knights of the North' Squadron, 1956
Thirteen of these TR.33 aircraft entered IAF service after being purchased from a British scrap dealer early in 1956. K-78, (*Krav* = fighter), served with the 'Knights of the North' Squadron, and these TR.33s were the most popular of the Mosquitoes to fly. Finish was the standard Blue/Brown/Light Grey scheme, but note the variation of the black and yellow Suez Stripes.

© M.D.Howley 2000

and near the Egyptian Air Bases in the Canal area. Complete surprise was achieved and at 17.00, Yael Finkelstein, (the only female on the mission and co-pilot of the lead Dakota), relayed the order to the Squadron for the jump to begin.

On hitting the ground, the paratroopers secured their position and prepared to assault the Pass. Part of these preparations was the clearing of a landing strip, initially for the use of Piper Cubs in the spotting and Casualty Evacuation role, but eventually to take larger aircraft on re-supply missions. The Egyptians quickly overcame their surprise and mounted a swift response, establishing strong defensive positions to take control of the Pass. During the first night, Nord Noratlas transports dropped further supplies plus Jeeps mounting recoilless cannons to the paratroopers.

Operation Kadesh

The following day the IDF struck across the Border into the north at Rafah and Gaza, the centre at Nitzana to Abu Ageila and in southern Sinai at Kuntilla, to attack the main Egyptian military concentrations. The southern attack, led by General Ariel Sharon, was to move through Natkhe and join the Paratroops at Mitla.

At 09.00 next morning, preparations to evacuate the men injured during the Mitla drop were interrupted when two Egyptian MiG-15s attacked the IDF positions hitting a Piper Cub and setting it on fire. The IAF had lost its first aircraft to enemy action. (When the hostilities subsided, the wreckage was air-lifted back to Israel under a Sikorsky S-55 helicopter). Combat Air Patrols (CAPs) had been launched by the IAF at first light however, but when these cleared the area, the Egyptians re-appeared, first

Above: Natural metal overall MD 450 Ouragan '28' of the 'Hornet' Sqn being made ready for flight by ground crew. On 31 October 1956, two Ouragans of this Squadron attacked the Egyptian Destroyer *Ibrahim-Al-Awal* with rockets and gunfire. Thirty minutes afterwards the vessel surrendered to the Israeli Navy. Note the black and yellow 'Suez Stripes' on the wings and rear fuselage.

Below: Dassault MD 450 Ouragan '29' of the 'Hornet' Squadron, Hatzor, October 1956. This was one of the Ouragans that had been painted in the standard IAF camouflage colours of Blue and Brown over Light Grey. The *sharkmouth* was a characteristic of many of the Ouragans of this Squadron. Note the Suez Campaign stripes on rear fuselage and wings. The aircraft i/d numbers were in white 30cm high stylised characters.

Left: MD Ouragan '42' of the 'Hornet' Sqn displaying the *sharkmouth* nose associated with this unit. The bottom of the mouth was painted red and the top painted black. Note the demarcation between the red and black areas, and the squadron badge on the fin top above the aircraft i/d numeral. Suez Campaign stripes are just visible on the rear fuselage.

with Vampires, apparently on a reconnaissance mission, and then attacks by MiGs at Mitla and on Sharon's Brigade.

By midday, the Paratroops were under heavy fire from the Egyptians who had been rushing supplies and reinforcements to the Pass through the night and morning. The IAF were cleared to attack and fifteen Ouragans, eighteen Mystères and four Meteors attacked Egyptian positions and supply convoys with bombs, rockets and cannon fire. Attacking in waves, the aircraft pounded the Egyptians for the next two hours.

Right: Flying shot of Dassault Mystère IVA '61' of 101 Sqn with Suez stripes around the rear fuselage. These aircraft were the leading IAF fighters of the Suez Campaign and operated in the Air Defence Role in addition to participating in ground-attack missions. Mystères claimed seven air-to-air kills - four DH Vampires and three MiG-15s.

Below: Dassault Mystère IVA '63' of 101 Sqn., based at Hatzor in October 1956. Overall natural metal finish with black and yellow Suez Campaign stripes around the wings and rear fuselage. The Squadron was reformed on the Mystère IVA on 1 April 1956. The individual aircraft i/d numeral '63' was in black 30cm high characters on the forward fuselage and on the fin. Note the 101 Sqn badge also on the fin.

To protect these ground attack missions, a further eight Mystères were sent on CAP missions near the Suez Canal. As some of these patrolling aircraft neared Kabrit Airfield, they spotted four MiG-15s and all eight Mystères grouped to attack. However, fearing a ground-attack strike against the airfield, the Egyptians scrambled a further twelve MiGs to intercept the Mystères, and improve the odds in their

favour. In the ensuing dog-fight, one MiG was shot down and another damaged. One Mystère was damaged before, low on fuel, they withdrew from the melée. The MiGs did not pursue. Ground-attack missions in support of all three thrusts into Sinai continued uninterrupted by the Egyptian Air Force.

At 03.30 the following morning, 31 October 1956, the Egyptian Navy Destroyer *Ibrahim-Al-Awal* closed on Haifa and fired 220 shells into the Israeli Navy Base, before heading away north towards Lebanon. At 05.30, the Israeli warships *Yaffo* and *Eilat* intercepted her, and aided by an IAF Dakota dropping flares, began firing as soon as she came into range. The Egyptian vessel began a series of evasive manoeuvres and the Navy called for further Air Force assistance.

At 06.00, two Ouragans piloted by Yaakov Agassi and David Kishon took off and headed for the scene. Both Ouragans, which the previous day had

Left: Boeing B-17G Flying Fortress '23', of 69 Squadron, based at Ramat David, in October 1956. When the Flying Fortresses were being made ready for action, aircraft '23' was due to receive full camouflage cover, but by the time of the action, only the IAF Brown uppersurface and Light Grey underside colours had been applied. Note that black and yellow Suez Campaign stripes had been applied to fuselage, (just infront of the numeral 23), and across the wings.

on the return home they spotted two further MiGs and gave chase. Nevo scored hits on one of the MiGs on his third attempt, and it was seen to fall away, eventually crashing into Badawill Lagoon, near the Sea. (This MiG was recovered by IAF ground crews and is now on display at Hazor Air Base). In the afternoon, an encounter with two further MiGs resulted in Nevo again sending one spiralling down into the sands.

The night of 31 October 1956 was a turning point, as the British and French put the first phase of 'Operation Musketeer' into effect with the bombing of Egyptian Airfields and other military targets. An order for Egyptian units to fall back from Sinai presented the IAF with long columns to attack, and with the achievement of the ground objectives IDF Army Units pursued the Egyptians to a point ten miles from the Canal Zone. The stopping point as agreed with the British and French Governments.

However actions continued throughout Sinai and the IDF still had other objectives to accomplish, such as opening the Straits of Tiran to Israeli shipping, and that meant taking the Egyptian positions at Sharm-El-Sheikh.

Sharm-El-Sheikh

Israeli Forces set out to capture Sharm-El-Sheikh on 1 November 1956. At the entrance to the Straits stood the fortification of Ras Natzrani, housing two large cannons with dominated the shipping channel. The following day, Egyptian positions, including this fortification, came under heavy bombing by the IAF who utilised Mustangs, Mosquitoes, B-17s, Ouragans and Mystères in the attack. In view of the Egyptian recall order, defences were expected to be minimal, but the IAF were met with dense anti-aircraft fire. Several

been attacking Egyptian armour, now used their armour-piercing rockets to telling effect on the Destroyer, and thirty minutes after the attack the *Ibrahim-Al-Awar* surrendered to the Israeli Navy.

Although the day had started well, the Israelis learned that Britain and France had postponed 'Operation Musketeer' and its opening strikes on Egyptian Airfields. Concern grew about growing air attacks on Israeli Forces and worse, possible attacks on Israeli cities. Over Mitla, four Egyptian Vampires were spotted by two Mystères of 101 Squadron, piloted by Shai Egozi and Yalo Shavit. The Mystères dived to attack with Egozi firing his cannons, first at the nearest Vampire which fell away, crashing into the desert below. Continuing the chase Egozi then fired at the second Vampire causing severe damage. As he pulled away, the pilot ejected. The remaining two Vampires broke left with Shavit giving chase and gradually gaining a position from where he fired a long bursts of his 30mm cannons, downing both aircraft.

Attacks on Egyptian armoured and supply convoys, as well as their fortifications, continued throughout the day, with Mustangs, Mosquitoes and even rocket-firing Harvards being particularly active. At night, the IAF mounted raids on Egyptian positions near Rafah using two B-17s accompanied by

Harvards dropping flares. However bad weather and poor visibility ruined any chance of success. Attempts by the Egyptian Air Force to counter these attacks also proved fruitless, although the presence of their MiGs could not be ignored. It was left to the Egyptian ground forces to protect themselves as best they could, and in several cases they proved quite effective, being able to put up a murderous barrage, particularly telling on the piston-engined Mustangs.

Eight Israeli aircraft had been shot down and a further twenty-one aircraft hit sustaining varying degrees of damage. Over Abu Ageila, an attack by six Ouragans was broken-up by a formation of eight MiG-15s which caused damage to two of the Ouragans and caused a third to force land back at its base.

The missions mounted by IAF Mystère pilots Yak Nevo and Yosef Tsuk were certainly eventful. On their morning patrol, they encountered a flight of three MiGs, but the action was inconclusive. However,

Right: North American P-51D Mustang of the 'Flying Wing' Squadron based at Tel Nof, October 1956. Standard IAF Blue and Brown over Light Grey camouflage scheme, with red spinner and white back plate which was a feature of this Squadron. (The 'Scorpion' Squadron painted their Mustang spinners yellow). Suez Campaign black and yellow stripe markings were applied to the wings and fuselage. This Mustang is being loaded with underwing rockets prior to another ground-attack mission.

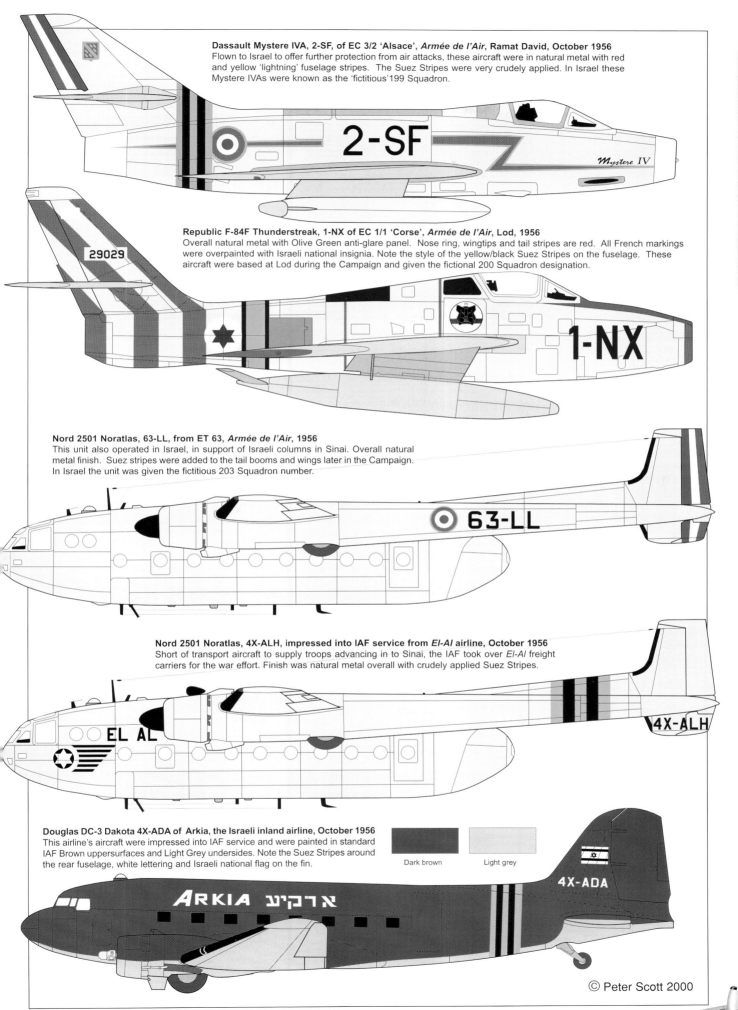

Dassault Mystere IVA, 2-SF, of EC 3/2 'Alsace', *Armée de l'Air*, Ramat David, October 1956
Flown to Israel to offer further protection from air attacks, these aircraft were in natural metal with red and yellow 'lightning' fuselage stripes. The Suez Stripes were very crudely applied. In Israel these Mystere IVAs were known as the 'fictitious' 199 Squadron.

Republic F-84F Thunderstreak, 1-NX of EC 1/1 'Corse', *Armée de l'Air*, Lod, 1956
Overall natural metal with Olive Green anti-glare panel. Nose ring, wingtips and tail stripes are red. All French markings were overpainted with Israeli national insignia. Note the style of the yellow/black Suez Stripes on the fuselage. These aircraft were based at Lod during the Campaign and given the fictional 200 Squadron designation.

Nord 2501 Noratlas, 63-LL, from ET 63, *Armée de l'Air*, 1956
This unit also operated in Israel, in support of Israeli columns in Sinai. Overall natural metal finish. Suez stripes were added to the tail booms and wings later in the Campaign. In Israel the unit was given the fictitious 203 Squadron number.

Nord 2501 Noratlas, 4X-ALH, impressed into IAF service from *El-Al* airline, October 1956
Short of transport aircraft to supply troops advancing in to Sinai, the IAF took over *El-Al* freight carriers for the war effort. Finish was natural metal overall with crudely applied Suez Stripes.

Douglas DC-3 Dakota 4X-ADA of Arkia, the Israeli inland airline, October 1956
This airline's aircraft were impressed into IAF service and were painted in standard IAF Brown uppersurfaces and Light Grey undersides. Note the Suez Stripes around the rear fuselage, white lettering and Israeli national flag on the fin.

Dark brown   Light grey

© Peter Scott 2000

Left: DH Mosquito FB.6 of the 'Knights of the North' Squadron, based at Ramat David, October 1956, being re-fuelled for further missions. Most operational Mosquitoes had been repainted in standard IAF Blue/Brown uppersurface camouflage with Light Grey undersides by the time of the Suez Campaign. Note the 'style' of the black and yellow Suez stripes on wings and fuselage - a broad yellow band, with narrower black stripes. Black spinners and rudder were generally applied to the Mosquitoes of this Squadron.

Opposite top: Gloster Meteor F.8 '08' of the 'First Jet' Squadron, temporarily based at Tel Nof, October 1956, in overall painted Aluminium finish. Rather than the standard yellow and black Suez Campaign markings, Meteors of the 'First Jet' Squadron sported a single black band around the rear fuselage and across the chord of the wing just outboard of the engine nacelle, the 'old style' cockpit canopy with the metal covering to the rear, and the Squadron badge on nose.

Opposite middle: AW Meteor NF.13 of the 'Bat' Squadron. In 1958, the IAF received two of the last three Meteor NF.13s it had ordered after the embargo imposed in 1956 was lifted. The third Meteor crashed en-route to Israel.

Opposite bottom: Gloster Meteor F.8 '02' of the 'First Jet Squadron' seen at Ramat David, in October 1956. Ramat David was the normal home base of this Meteor Squadron, which moved to Tel Nof during the Suez Campaign. This aircraft is in painted Aluminium overall finish and has the full clear canopy. Again note the Squadron badge on nose, which was applied to both sides.

aircraft were damaged and the IAF lost their only Mystère IV of the Campaign when Benny Peled, later to command the IAF, was forced to eject when his Mystère was hit and caught fire. He was subsequently rescued by a Piper Cub and flown back to Israel.

In support of the ground forces moving from Eilat, the IDF launched an airborne assault on the airfield at A-Tur, close to Shar-El-Sheikh on the Red Sea. Ten IAF Dakotas dropped the paratroopers over their objectives and within a short time, the airfield was ready for use by the IAF. An *El-Al* Constellation ferrying IAF technicians and equipment was one of the first aircraft to land.

Action against Egyptian Forces continued with one of their transport ships, spotted off the Straits, being attacked and sunk by a formation of Mystères. Following this attack, a second formation of Mystères also spotted a warship nearby and attacked it with rockets, causing considerable damage. However, this was the British Destroyer *HMS Crane* whose presence was unknown to the Israelis.

With a United Nations cease-fire looming, the IDF was keen to accomplish all its objectives before it came into effect. Reconnaissance missions were launched, involving Mosquito PR 16s for a French F-84 Thunderstreak attack on Luxor Air Base, and B-17s which spent considerable time over the Straits accurately pinpointing the Egyptian positions. Air and ground assaults on these positions began to take their toll and on 6 November 1956, the Egyptians surrendered. The United Nations cease-fire came into effect on 8 November 1956.

Cease fire

Israel was pleased with its achievements and proud of its Air Force which had accomplished all that had been promised, and vindicated the commanders who never doubted its capability and influence in battle. The IAF flew nearly 1900 sorties, of which nearly five hundred were attacks on ground targets. In fifteen air-to-air engagements, the IAF shot down seven Egyptian aircraft. Egypt had only one aerial victory, a Piper Cub, which was shot down after being attacked by MiG-15s. Ground fire had taken the heaviest toll - the IAF lost nine Mustangs, two Harvards and a single Mystère.

Below: Gloster Meteor FR.9 '37', of the 'First Jet' Squadron, based at Ramat David, photographed just after the 1956 Suez Campaign. The FR.9s served in the ground-attack role with the Meteor F.8s, and were painted in the standard IAF Blue/Brown uppersurfaces with Light Grey undersurfaces camouflage scheme. Note that the nose tip camera window was painted-over as were the fuselage side camera windows, and that the cannon port area was painted black - albeit peeling away.

Chapter 4
The Decade of Calm

New thinking
New equipment

Following the Suez Campaign, the IAF was looked upon in a new light. It had proved itself to be a capable force in the defence of Israel, demonstrating its air superiority over the battlefront, in close support and in the transportation of troops and equipment.

Shortcomings had been recognised and lessons learned. Many aircraft used during the Campaign were old and vulnerable piston-engined types, such as the P-51D Mustang, which were proving unsuitable for the modern battlefield. More modern types such as the Ouragan proved themselves to be stable gun platforms, reliable in close support work and able to take a lot of punishment by ground fire whilst remaining airworthy. The Israeli Ministry of Defence was now listening to the Air Force which was to enter a phase of modernisation, in training, communications, bases and equipment. The year 1956 was also the 'swansong' of the B-17s, P-51D Mustangs and Mosquitoes, as they were all phased out of service after the Campaign.

What the Campaign did show was the need for better supply and casualty evacuation provisions and the potential of the helicopter for this role. On 10 November 1956, the 'Flying Elephant' Transport Squadron Helicopter Flight was formed at Tel Nof with two Sikorsky S-55s

Heading: The arrival of additional Dassault MD 450 Ouragans from France in the mid 1960s enabled the IAF to form a new Squadron, the 'Lion's Head' Squadron. Ouragan '92' was allocated to this squadron and their badge can just be made out on the fin. The standard IAF camouflage of Blue and Brown uppersurfaces with Light Grey undersides was well established by this period.

Below: Out with the old and in with the new! A Sud Vautour IIA '25' of the 'Knights of the North' Squadron receiving its Blue/Brown camouflage paint during 1958. In the background can be seen two former IAF types, a Curtiss C-46 Commando, long since transferred from the IAF to the Israeli national airline _El Al_, and a Consolidated PBY-5A Catalina withdrawn from service in 1956.

Right: In November 1956, a Helicopter Flight was established with the Nords in the 'Elephant' Squadron. This Flight comprised a Hiller 360 and two Sikorsky S-55 Helicopters '02' and '03'. This photograph of a Sikorsky S-55 in fact represents '03' and is currently on display at the Israeli Air Force Museum. Before the Flight was established, the real '03' was used at the end of the Suez Campaign to ferry the damaged Piper Cub From Mitla back to Israel.

and a Hiller 360. Its task was to train helicopter crews for the IAF and to develop helicopter operations in support of all IDF activities. The S-55s painted in the Blue/Brown standard camouflage colours, and serialled '02' and '03', were equipped with the more powerful Wright R-1300-R engine and had the additional smaller windows along the fuselage sides.

As more pilots were converted to the Mystère IV, a second operator, the 'Valley' Squadron was formed at Ramat David on 16 December 1956. This Squadron had formerly operated Mosquitoes. A new Squadron badge of a Bird over a Crescent Moon, on a blue background, adorned the tail of their aircraft as it soon moved to operational status.

The biggest change in 1956 was the decision to move to a modern all jet force, with an emphasis on quality and the procurement of the best the country could afford to meet its needs. One important step to the implementation of this policy was the selection of the jet powered Fouga Magister as the future

Right: In the early 1960s, training on the Fouga Magister began in the IAF. Fouga '65' was one of the first produced with French help by Bedek Aviation. Originally the Fougas entered service in natural metal, but were soon camouflaged, except for the Yellow trainer markings on the nose, tail and wing tips.

Below: Fouga Magister '16' painted in the standard IAF Blue/Brown camouflage at the Flight School in the early 1960s. The Fougas replaced the Harvards, (one can be seen behind the tail), and offered jet training after an initial course on Piper Super Cubs.

training aircraft of the IAF. One example of the Magister arrived at the Bedek Aviation Co, (now Israeli Aircraft Industries), where local production of the airframes was to begin, although it would be another three years before the type entered IAF service.

The IAF knew it would never be able to match its adversaries in aircraft quantity, so its success would lie in the quality of its pilots and equipment. The procurement of the Mystère IV was the start of that policy, but pilot conversion training to all modern types was slow

and the aircraft were not being operated to their full potential. As a consequence, IAF pilots were sent to France to gain operational experience with Armée de l'Air units, many returning with instructor qualifications to teach others the benefits of their experience.

The close links with France had an unexpected effect when, on 25 July 1957, the Helicopter Flight gained a new SA Alouette II, donated by Madame de la Meurthe and flown to Tel Nof in an IAF Nord Noratlas.

More Jet Fighters

The Mosquito had proved itself a capable multi-role aircraft and with its withdrawal from service, the IAF set about looking for a replacement. With the close relationship developed with France, it was natural that their aircraft industry would be considered first. The chosen replacement was the Sud Aviation Vautour. In 1956 a mixture of Vautour variants were selected comprising, seventeen Vautour IIA single-seat attack aircraft, seven Vautour IIN two-seat night-fighter aircraft, and four Vautour IIBs two-seat bombers converted for reconnaissance duties in Israel.

Deliveries of the Vautour IIAs began with the first of the type arriving in Israel on 1 August 1957, and going straight into storage at Hatzor until crews had completed their conversion training.

The 'Knights of the North' Squadron, previously a Mosquito Unit, was reformed at Ramat David on 19 January 1958 to operate the Vautour IIAs and IIBs. The Vautour IINs joined the Meteor equipped 'Bat' Squadron, the first four aircraft arriving on 4 April 1958. This Squadron had also just received two Meteor NF 13s embargoed since 1956. A third aircraft had crashed en-route. Deliveries of the Vautours were completed by April 1959. All of them were in natural metal, except for the light grey electronic equipment 'spine' on the top of the aircraft and the light tan radar nose-cone of the IIN version.

On 4 December 1958, four new SMBD Super Mystère B2s arrived in Israel to equip the reformed 'Scorpion' Squadron at Hatzor, which was to receive all of the twenty-four aircraft purchased. First tested in France the previous year by veteran IAF pilot Yak Nevo, he was very impressed with the Super Mystère's performance and recommended the type to the IAF, particularly to counter the MiG-19 'Farmer' entering service with Arab Air Arms. Powered by the Atar 101 engine, the Super Mystère was Europe's first supersonic fighter. It was to spend all its IAF service with one Squadron, who lost

no time in adorning their new natural metal finished aircraft with a red 'Lightning Flash' along each fuselage side. As the Super Mystère took over the leading interceptor role, the Mystère IV was re-designated in to the ground-attack role and began to receive the standard Blue/Brown over Light Grey camouflage scheme, which was also being applied to the Ouragan and Vautour Fleets.

Although a standard camouflage pattern of Blue and Brown uppersurfaces and Light Grey undersurfaces existed for all aircraft to be painted in, a new pattern was to become standard for swept-wing aircraft which was different to that applied to straight-winged aircraft such as Mustangs and Ouragans. The new pattern was first painted on Mystère IVs and then Vautours. However, as before, there were variations, again where the colours were reversed and in some cases, aircraft were painted in a 'mirror' image of the standard/reversed patterns.

Improved helicopters

To boost helicopter support, three Sikorsky S-58s had been delivered by ship from the United States to join the

S-55s in the newly formed 'Rolling Swords' Squadron, whose badge showed three swirling Scimitar sword blades. The Sikorsky S-58s were purchased as civil machines and adapted to suit IAF service, including the application of camouflage colours.

Left: Sud Vautour IIA '15' of the 'Knights of the North' Squadron, at Ramat David in 1958. The Squadron was formed on 19 January that year, although many of their aircraft had been in storage at Hatzor until enough crews had been trained.

Above: Sud Vautour IIN '61' of the 'Bat' Squadron, which received its first four new aircraft in April 1958. This Squadron was the IAF's only Night Fighter unit and operated their Vautours alongside their Meteor NF.13s.

They could carry a heavier payload than the S-55s and were more versatile, being better suited to hot and high areas of operation.

In July 1958, another IAF veteran pilot, Major General Ezer Weizman, took over as IAF Commander, overseeing the modernisation of the Force and instilling his own standards of professionalism. Under his command the IAF was to emerge as a coherent organisation with a 'family' spirit. All the Branches and Units within the IAF were brought closer together, each having an important contribution to the overall success of the missions. Aircraft turn-around times for re-fuelling and re-arming were

Below: Two Dassault Super Mystère B2s over the sea. In December 1958 the IAF took delivery of the first of twenty-four ordered SMBD Super Mystère B2s, reforming the 'Scorpion' Squadron at Hatzor to operate this type. They soon adorned their aircraft with the striking red lightning fuselage stripe.

dramatically reduced, increasing aircraft mission availability.

MiG-17 ambush

As the Super Mystère began entering service, an action took place over Sinai on 20 December 1958 between IAF Mystère IVs and Egyptian MiG-17s, resulting in the shooting down of one of the MiGs. In a carefully staged ambush, patrolling MiG-17s from El Arish airbase in Sinai, were lured towards a quartet of Mystère IVs led by Yak Nevo. As they approached, the Mystère flight split into two, with one pair clearing the area, and the other ready to strike.

When the strike pair of Mystères were spotted, the MiGs turned away. Yak and his wingman gave chase, and having the advantage of surprise and height, soon gaining on the trailing MiG-17. Yak opened fire with his two 30mm Defa cannons, and hits were seen on the MiG's right wing and fuselage. After Yak had expended nearly all of his

Above: Sikorsky S-58 of the 'Rolling Swords' Squadron circa late 1958. The IAF acquired six Sikorsky S-58s from the United States during 1958 and formed this new Squadron to replace the 'Elephant' Squadron Helicopter Flight, established two years earlier.

ammunition, the MiG pilot was seen to eject, the abandoned aircraft impacting into the desert sands. Yak was to try to repeat his ambush success the following year.

At noon on 4 November 1959, Yak, this time flying a Super Mystère B2, after being appointed commander of the 'Scorpion' Squadron, repeated his flight near the Egyptian border over southern Israel, again trying to entice the Egyptians at Al Arish into combat. Four MiG-17s accepted the challenge as they crossed over into Israeli air space, chasing the 'bait' of two of the Super Mystères, (led by David Ivri, later to command the IAF), flying low and slow to their front. As the MiGs crossed, Yak and his wingman broke into them from above

Dassault MD 450 Ouragan '70', of the 'Hornet' Squadron, 1957
Following the Suez Campaign, the process of applying the IAF standard camouflage colours of Blue and Brown uppersurfaces and Light Grey undersides to the Ouragans was renewed. Soon after the Campaign, the Suez recognition stripes were removed. The *sharkmouth* became a characteristic for this Squadron's Ouragans, note that the red area of the mouth is the lower section.

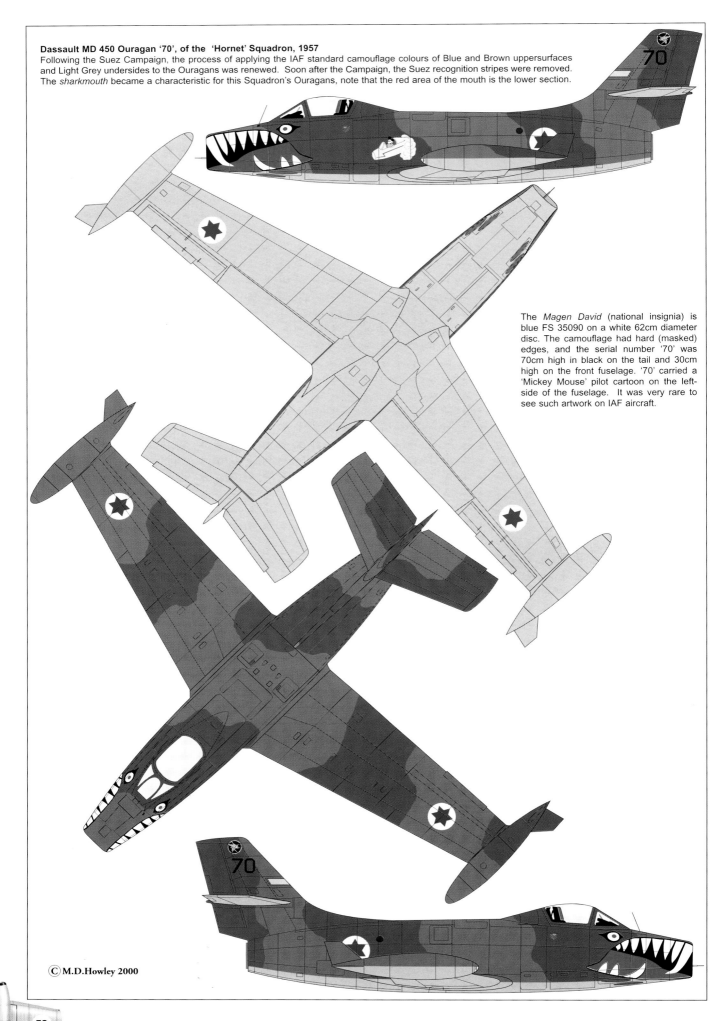

The *Magen David* (national insignia) is blue FS 35090 on a white 62cm diameter disc. The camouflage had hard (masked) edges, and the serial number '70' was 70cm high in black on the tail and 30cm high on the front fuselage. '70' carried a 'Mickey Mouse' pilot cartoon on the left-side of the fuselage. It was very rare to see such artwork on IAF aircraft.

© M.D.Howley 2000

Dassault MD 450 Ouragan '94' of the 'Winged Lion's Head' Squadron late 1950s
The acquisition of further ex-French Air Force Ouragans in 1957 enabled the IAF to form a second Ouragan Squadron. By this time the fuselage serial number had been increased in size and was painted white. The camouflage scheme was still the standard Blue/Brown/Light Grey.

Dassault Mystere IVA '47', of the 'Valley' Squadron, Ramat David, late-1950s
The 'Valley' Squadron has a badge showing a black bird of prey on a crescent moon with a blue background. The camouflage scheme is the standard IAF Blue/Brown/Light Grey. The serial number '47' is in white.

Dassault Super Mystere B2, '17' of the 'Scorpion' Squadron, 1958
The Squadron, a former Spitfire and Mustang operator in the Operational Training role, was re-formed at Hatzor on 4 December 1958 to operate the Super Mystere, and was the only IAF Squadron to do so. The aircraft was well liked for its capacity to take on the MiG-19, then entering service in Egypt. The red lightning flash became a characteristic of this Squadron.

Sud-Aviation Vautour IIN '62' of the 'Bat' Squadron, 1958
Chosen as a Mosquito replacement, seven Vautour IINs were acquired by the IAF with deliveries starting in April 1958. The Squadron operated these aircraft in natural metal alongside the Meteor NF.13. The SNCASO logo was retained on the fin of these aircraft, whilst they were operated in natural metal. The nose radar cone was in a dark grey moulded fibre glass material.

Sud-Aviation Vautour IIB '33' of the 'Knights of the North' Squadron, late 1950s
Four Vautour IIBs were acquired by the IAF and converted to IIBR standard with a photo-reconnaissance capability. The Squadron badge is a bird carrying a rocket on a blue background. Note Vautour name logo on the nose.

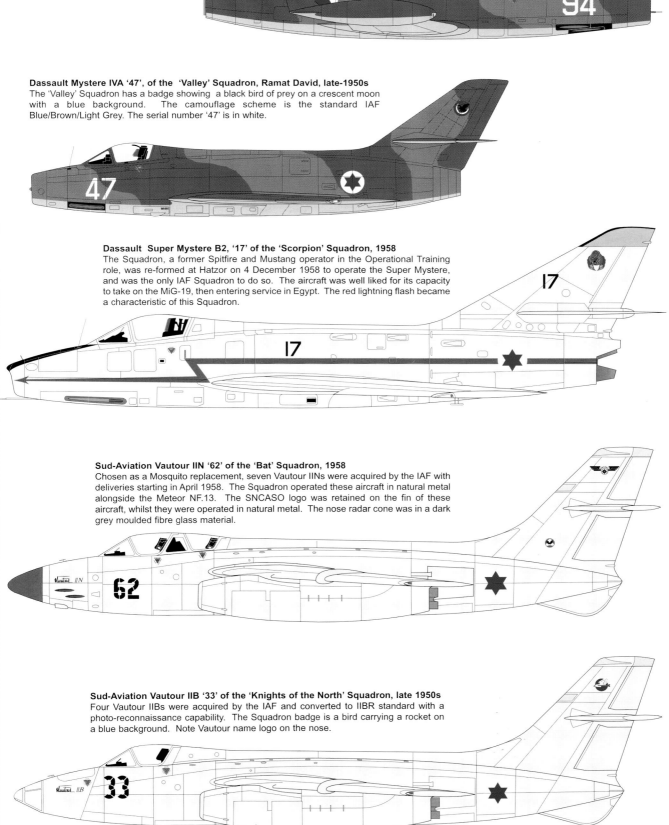

© M.D.Howley 2000

and behind. One MiG was hit, but all four quickly cleared to area returning to base. The incident also had a cost to the Israelis, as Ivri had problems with his Super Mystère as he turned to rejoin the formation for the flight home. Control was lost and he entered into a tight spin from which he could not recover, and was forced to eject. He was soon rescued by a Sikorsky S-58 and flown back to base.

New training procedures

During 1959, a major review of flying training procedures took place when only

one candidate at the Flying School received his 'wings'. At this time, basic training took place on Boeing Stearman Kaydets, before moving to advanced training on Harvards. Pilots destined to fly fighters then went for operational training on Ouragans. Training was also available on Meteor T 7s, particularly for those earmarked to fly Vautours.

New procedures and a new syllabus was introduced, including a preliminary stage on Piper Super Cubs, an Officer Training course, and then further flying stages on Harvards, which were about to be replaced by the Fouga Magister. Advanced training was with the 'First Jet' Squadron on Meteors. By 1962 basic and advanced training was undertaken completely on jet aircraft. Ouragans were still used in the Fighter Operational Training role.

SM B2's first 'air-to-air'

The Super Mystères were in action again over Israel's southern border when, on 28 April 1961 a Flight of two aircraft tangled with four Egyptian MiG-17s over Nitzana. As they turned into each other, Super Mystère pilot Tzur Ben-Barak scored hits along the wing and fuselage of a MiG from which the pilot was seen to eject. This was the first air to air combat victory for the Super Mystère and the 'Scorpion' Squadron.

The Mirage

Although the Super Mystère was Israel's lead interceptor at the start of the 1960s, its service entry was overshadowed by events in France, and the IAF's preparations for the entry of a truly modern supersonic fighter. Dassault had been developing a

Above: Dassault Ouragan '61' of the 'Hornet' Squadron. These aircraft had performed well during the Suez Campaign, but they were always overshadowed by the Dassault Mystére IVA. Note the red lightning flash on the wing tip fuel tank.

Left: The process of camouflaging the Ouragans of the 'Hornet' Squadron continued after the Suez campaign but the *sharkmouth* was retained. Ouragan '70' was one of only a handful to sport artwork - a Mickey-Mouse cartoon can just be seen on the mid fuselage just below the rear of the open canopy.

supersonic delta wing jet fighter to counter the threats posed by the emerging new MiGs and Sukhois from the Soviet Union.

Utilising the power of the new SNECMA Atar engines, the Mirage III was capable of Mach 2. Its looks and performance soon captivated the IAF. In the spring of 1959, Israeli test pilot Danny Shapira demonstrated the Mirage to Ezer Weizman, who recommended the type for the IAF. A contract soon followed for seventy-two single-seat fighters and four two-seat trainers. These aircraft were to be configured to IAF specifications, which included the provision of a gun armament in addition to the bombs and missiles it had been designed to carry. The Israeli version was designated Mirage IIICJ, the J standing for

Below: Gloster Meteor T.7 '17' and Gloster Meteor T.71/2 '21' - (a T.7 with an F.8 tail unit!), of the 'Knights of the North' Squadron, camouflaged in the standard IAF Blue/Brown/Light Grey scheme with white numerals. Note the 'Knights of the North' squadron badge on the tops of the fin/rudder. These aircraft were used to train pilots destined to fly the various Marks of Sud Vautour II.

'Juif' the French word for Jew.

On 7 April 1962, Danny Shapira delivered the first of the Mirage IIIs to Israel landing at Hatzor on the *Sabbath*. The welcoming ceremony was put off until the Sunday to avoid disrespect to the Jewish *Sabbath*. (NB: Fourteen years later in 1976, the delivery ceremony for the MD F-15 Eagle went over into the Jewish *Sabbath*, and the Religious Parties in the Coalition Government walked out at the disrespect, collapsing the Government!).

Three Squadrons were reformed to operate the Mirage IIICJ.
●The 'First Jet' Squadron, previously operated Meteor F 8s and FR 9s at Ramat David. A red stripe was painted along the fuselage sides of their aircraft.
●101 Squadron, which gave up its Mystère IV aircraft to operate Mirages at

Hatzor. As with previous aircraft on this Squadron, the rudders were painted with red and white diagonal stripes.
●The 'Bat' Squadron which gave up its Vautour IINs to operate Mirages at Tel Nof. This Squadron painted a red chevron on each side of the fin leading edge.
All three Squadrons kept their aircraft very clean and highly polished.

The Mystère IVs went to the 'Flying Wing' Squadron, which was the last unit to operate the P-51D Mustang. The Vautour IINs were converted from use as night fighters into two-seat bombers and allocated to the 'Knights of the North' Squadron which continued to operate them alonside its Vautour IIAs.

Further changes
These were not the only aircraft changes at the time. The 'Scorpion' Squadron

Above: In April 1962, the IAF took delivery of the first of 72 Dassault Mirage IIICJs. Mirage '409' was one of the first to be delivered and served with 101 Squadron which had converted from the Mystère IVA. The aircraft were left in their natural metal finish with black nose radomes and red intake trimming. The squadron's red/white striped rudder had yet to be painted on this aircraft.

Below: Line-up of Dassault Mystère IVAs of 101 Sqn at Hatzor. In December 1958 these aircraft clashed with Egyptian MiG-17s over Sinai and succeeded in shooting down one of the MiGs. Note the mixture of natural metal and Blue/Brown camouflage schemes.

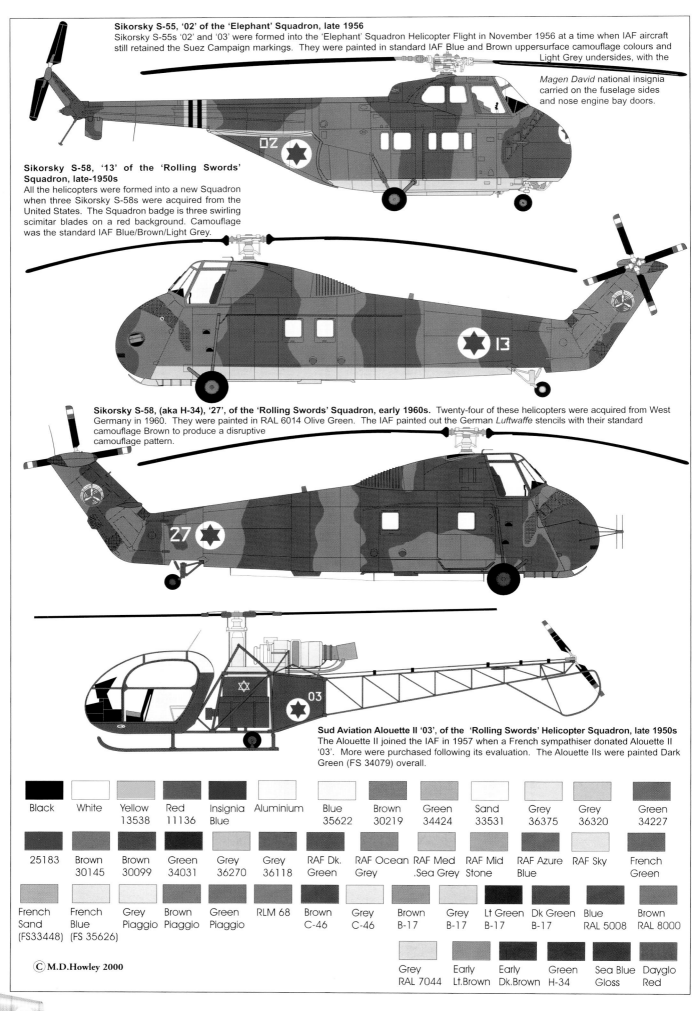

Sikorsky S-55, '02' of the 'Elephant' Squadron, late 1956
Sikorsky S-55s '02' and '03' were formed into the 'Elephant' Squadron Helicopter Flight in November 1956 at a time when IAF aircraft still retained the Suez Campaign markings. They were painted in standard IAF Blue and Brown uppersurface camouflage colours and Light Grey undersides, with the

Magen David national insignia carried on the fuselage sides and nose engine bay doors.

Sikorsky S-58, '13' of the 'Rolling Swords' Squadron, late-1950s
All the helicopters were formed into a new Squadron when three Sikorsky S-58s were acquired from the United States. The Squadron badge is three swirling scimitar blades on a red background. Camouflage was the standard IAF Blue/Brown/Light Grey.

Sikorsky S-58, (aka H-34), '27', of the 'Rolling Swords' Squadron, early 1960s. Twenty-four of these helicopters were acquired from West Germany in 1960. They were painted in RAL 6014 Olive Green. The IAF painted out the German *Luftwaffe* stencils with their standard camouflage Brown to produce a disruptive camouflage pattern.

Sud Aviation Alouette II '03', of the 'Rolling Swords' Helicopter Squadron, late 1950s
The Alouette II joined the IAF in 1957 when a French sympathiser donated Alouette II '03'. More were purchased following its evaluation. The Alouette IIs were painted Dark Green (FS 34079) overall.

Black	White	Yellow 13538	Red 11136	Insignia Blue	Aluminium	Blue 35622	Brown 30219	Green 34424	Sand 33531	Grey 36375	Grey 36320	Green 34227

25183	Brown 30145	Brown 30099	Green 34031	Grey 36270	Grey 36118	RAF Dk. Green	RAF Ocean Grey	RAF Med .Sea Grey	RAF Mid Stone	RAF Azure Blue	RAF Sky	French Green

French Sand (FS33448)	French Blue (FS 35626)	Grey Piaggio	Brown Piaggio	Green Piaggio	RLM 68	Brown C-46	Grey C-46	Brown B-17	Grey B-17	Lt Green B-17	Dk Green B-17	Blue RAL 5008	Brown RAL 8000

Grey RAL 7044	Early Lt.Brown	Early Dk.Brown	Green H-34	Sea Blue Gloss	Dayglo Red

© M.D.Howley 2000

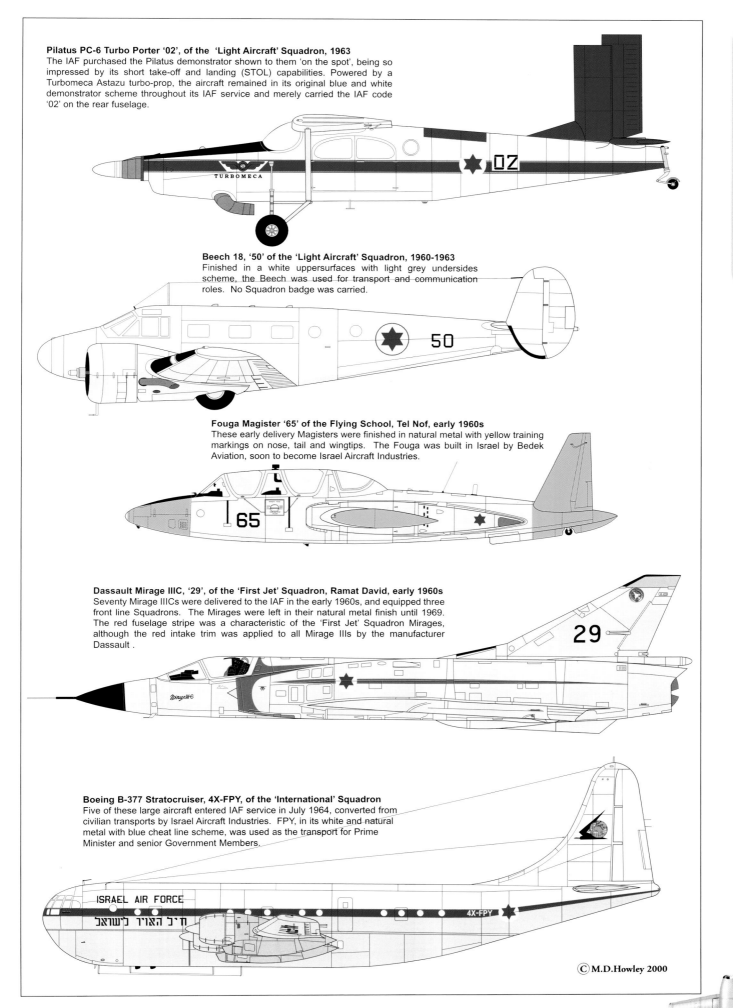

Pilatus PC-6 Turbo Porter '02', of the 'Light Aircraft' Squadron, 1963
The IAF purchased the Pilatus demonstrator shown to them 'on the spot', being so impressed by its short take-off and landing (STOL) capabilities. Powered by a Turbomeca Astazu turbo-prop, the aircraft remained in its original blue and white demonstrator scheme throughout its IAF service and merely carried the IAF code '02' on the rear fuselage.

Beech 18, '50' of the 'Light Aircraft' Squadron, 1960-1963
Finished in a white uppersurfaces with light grey undersides scheme, the Beech was used for transport and communication roles. No Squadron badge was carried.

Fouga Magister '65' of the Flying School, Tel Nof, early 1960s
These early delivery Magisters were finished in natural metal with yellow training markings on nose, tail and wingtips. The Fouga was built in Israel by Bedek Aviation, soon to become Israel Aircraft Industries.

Dassault Mirage IIIC, '29', of the 'First Jet' Squadron, Ramat David, early 1960s
Seventy Mirage IIICs were delivered to the IAF in the early 1960s, and equipped three front line Squadrons. The Mirages were left in their natural metal finish until 1969. The red fuselage stripe was a characteristic of the 'First Jet' Squadron Mirages, although the red intake trim was applied to all Mirage IIIs by the manufacturer Dassault .

Boeing B-377 Stratocruiser, 4X-FPY, of the 'International' Squadron
Five of these large aircraft entered IAF service in July 1964, converted from civilian transports by Israel Aircraft Industries. FPY, in its white and natural metal with blue cheat line scheme, was used as the transport for Prime Minister and senior Government Members.

© M.D.Howley 2000

Left: To assist with helicopter pilot training, the IAF purchased thirteen Bell 47 helicopters during 1965. With the purchase of more Sikorsky S-58s from Germany and the impending introduction of the Super Frelon, the IAF was going to need more helicopter pilots in the future.

Below: Pilatus PC-6 Turbo-Porter. The Short Take Off and Landing (STOL) capabilities of this aircraft so impressed the IAF that two were immediately purchased. Given IAF serial numbers, (02 is shown here), the aircraft retained their civil white and blue colour scheme.

Bottom: Fouga Magister '212' of the Aerobatic Team. Flown by instructors, the Fougas of the aerobatic team began to thrill the Israeli crowds during the 1960s. They were painted dark blue overall with white stripes outlined in red.

received an additional twelve Super Mystères. With the introduction of the Mirage, the Super Mystères were painted the standard Blue/Brown/Light Grey camouflage scheme.

Also in 1962 an agreement was signed with West Germany which included the delivery of further aircraft into the IAF. These included:-

• Twelve Nord Noratlas Transports which entered service with the 'Elephant' Squadron. (An additional four aircraft were ordered later)

• Twenty-four Sikorsky H-34 helicopters for the 'Rolling Swords' Squadron. Unlike their six current US standard H-34s, the German examples had a different engine exhaust system on the left of the nose, different undercarriage attachments and different internal equipment. They were also painted in the standard German RAL 6014 Olive Green colour. Rather than repainting them in the Blue and Brown standard IAF colours, the IAF merely painted over the German stencil information with the Brown shade, giving a unique Olive Green and Brown camouflage pattern to these helicopters.

• Additional Fouga Magister trainers.

Heinkel had already been supplying complete wings to Bedek Aviation to help speed up production in Israel

• Twelve Dornier Do 27 high wing single-engined light aircraft for use as a liaison aircraft, painted in the standard Blue/Brown over Light Grey camouflage scheme. Delivery began in 1964 to the 'Flying Camel' Squadron.

At the same time as these aircraft were being delivered, the Swiss company Pilatus demonstrated their new PC-6 Turbo Porter to the Israeli Ministry of Defence. The Israelis were very

impressed with the Turbo Porter's load carrying capability and its Short Take-Off and Landing (STOL) performance, seeing it as a modern Noordyn Norseman. Two aircraft were immediately purchased. Unlike other IAF aircraft, the Turbo Porter was not camouflaged, and retained its overall white colouring with light-blue fuselage stripe, wing tips and fin.

Mirage modifications

As the Squadrons worked up on the Mirage to become fully operational, their delta wings became a familiar sight over

Above: Dassault Mirage IIICJ '915' of 101 Squadron. In April 1967, IAF Mirages supported an operation against Syrian artillery positions which were shelling Israeli settlements. By the end of the day the Mirages had shot down six Syrian MiGs without loss.

Israel. They soon took their place in the Order of Battle, flying patrols and maintaining a constant alert status. In July 1963, Mirages were scrambled to intercept an unidentified aircraft flying at high altitude over the country. As the Mirages closed the distance and altitude, they identified the aircraft as a USAF Martin RB-57 Reconnaissance Aircraft, which was then escorted to land at Lod Airport. After diplomatic discussions the aircraft was allowed to depart for Cyprus.

Occasionally the Mirages came into contact with aircraft from the Arab States, but these rarely escalated into clashes. On 20 August 1963, two Mirages did clash with eight Syrian MiG-17s, damaging two of them before both sides were forced to break away.

Dassault were becoming increasingly concerned about the Mirage, for although it had not happened with the IAF aircraft, seven Mirages had crashed due to engine problems. It was Israel's turn on 11 October 1963. On this day, IAF pilot Ran Ronen, had just completed a reconnaissance mission over Egyptian Airfields in the Nile Delta and was beginning his landing approach at Hatzor, when his engine lost power. Ran steered the Mirage to a nearby field and ejected at 400 feet. By a stroke of luck, the disabled Mirage glided down into the soft field to land virtually intact. Ran

Right: Dassault Mirage IIICJ '755' of 101 Squadron. On 14 July 1966, Mirages from this Squadron clashed with Syrian MiG 21s over the Golan Heights and Captain Yoram Agmon in Mirage '59' scored the type's first air-to-air victory, shooting down a MiG with his cannons.

recovered the film from the nose cameras, and Dassault engineers were allowed to examine the Mirage for the cause of the engine failure. This was found to be a fuel supply problem which Dassault could rectify to overcome. The IAF was reward by Dassault for their assistance and the crashed Mirage was soon repaired and returned to service.

This Mirage, number '53', of 101 Squadron was a standard Mirage IIICJ with an Israeli modified nose cone housing a wide angle camera for low level reconnaissance missions. Altogether, the IAF developed six different camera nose cones for use on Mirage IIICJs, each designed for a particular function or for use at different altitudes. On 10 March 1964, the IAF took delivery of two reconnaissance dedicated Mirage IIIRJs. Given the numbers '98' and '99', these were allocated to the 'Bat' Squadron at Tel Nof.

The Water War
In 1964 Israel finished construction of a National Water Carrier, designed to take water from the Sea of Galilee in the north to meet the needs of Towns and agricultural settlements in the south. The neighbouring Arab States vowed to disrupt the supply of water by damming and diverting the rivers that fed into northern Israel, supplying the Water Carrier. Israel obviously viewed this as a provocative act, and when Syria began constructing earthworks, troops from both sides took up positions to protect their water projects, and fighting inevitably ensued.

Border disputes and the Syrian shelling of Northern Settlements from the Golan Heights were a common occurrence, but both sides realised that this could lead to something much more serious, and on 13 November 1964 the IAF became involved.

Syrian troops attacked Israeli positions along the River Dan, supported by artillery fire from the Golan Heights which was also directed onto other Israeli positions and nearby settlements. The IAF was asked to intervene by bombing the Syrian positions. At Ramat David,

bombs were loaded on to Mystère IVs, Vautours and the Mirages and the aircraft despatched to assigned targets. The resulting bombardment, the first bomb-carrying action for both the Vautours and the Mirages, was a complete success and the Syrians broke off their action. Seeing the resolve of Israel to protect its water supply, many Arab countries withdrew their support for further confrontation, fearing a major war. Syria was to continue further action on its own and it was not long before clashes took place again.

Range-finding radar problem
The following day two Mirage IIICJs from 101 Squadron patrolling the Northern Border with Syria, were directed towards a flight of MiG-21s spotted in their area. Approaching from behind, the Mirage Flight Leader, Captain Amos Amir fired a Matra R-530 radar guided missile at a MiG. The missile failed to achieve a 'lock' and fell away. He then tried a *Shafrir 1* infra red homing missile, (an AIM 9 Sidewinder-type missile), but this too missed and dropped away. Having closed the range on the MiG-21, at 400 metres he fired his 30mm cannons and saw hits on the MiG. However, it broke away and Amir had to be content with a 'damaged' claim. This was the Mirage's first air-to-air combat encounter and the first operational firing of the Matra and *Shafrir 1* missiles.

A problem was detected in the Mirage radar which in Israeli service became predominantly used for range-finding purposes, but only after an alignment problem between the radar and the gunsight had been discovered and rectified.

Mirage 'air-to-airs'
Success was to come on 14 July 1966. Again the IAF was called to action following a clash between Israeli and Syrian ground forces over Syria's continued work on water diversion projects. Vautours and Mystère IVs bombed Syrian positions and engineering plant, whilst Mirages flew high altitude cover. Late in the afternoon, two MiG-

21s were seen flying over the Golan Heights heading towards the fighting and Mirage pilot Captain Yoram Agmon of 101 Squadron, turned to engage them.

Although the gunsight problem had been discovered, Agmon's Mirage IIICJ, number '59' which was destined to become the top scoring Mirage, had yet to be modified. Agmon's first shots all missed, and as a classic dogfight ensued it was not until he positioned himself almost 200 metres directly behind a MiG's tail that he scored hits, causing the it to enter a spin from which it could not recover. The Syrian pilot was seen to eject and parachute down to safety over his own territory. This was the first air-to-air victory for the Mirage, and the fact that it had been achieved over a MiG-21 delighted the French celebrating *Bastille Day*.

This success was repeated four weeks later, when on 15 August 1956, Mirages from the 'First Jet' Squadron were providing top cover for a mission to rescue the crew of an Israeli Patrol Boat which had run aground on the Syrian side of the Sea of Galilee. The patrol Boat came under Syrian air attack and ground forces had already shot down a MiG-17 before the Mirages intervened to provide top cover. But, the MiG-17s had their own cover of MiG-21s and the Mirages were soon in action. Mirage pilot Captain Yahuda Koren positioned himself behind a MiG-21 and fired a *Shafrir* which missed, before switching to his 30mm cannons. Again the range-finding sights on his aircraft had not been adjusted, and it was not until he fired from close range that his shells struck home as intended. The MiG burst into flames and crashed.

More new types
Whilst these northern fighter Squadrons were in action, changes took place in other parts of the IAF. A new air base opened at Hatzerim, with the flying school taking up residency in 1966.

Dwarfing all other aircraft in the IAF inventory, the Boeing B-377 Stratocruiser Transport started to enter service in July 1964. Five commercial

Above: Nord Noratlas 4X-FAD showing the Blue/Brown camouflage to good effect. After the Suez campaign in October 1956, the Nords, all serving with the 'Elephant' Squadron, began to be painted in the standard Israeli Air Force camouflage scheme. This was the start of the IAF's 'French Period' and Nords were frequent visitors to that country. For 'civvie' fans, note the BEA Viscount in the background.

variants had been acquired in 1962 and these had been converted for IAF use by Israeli Aircraft Industries, two of these aircraft being equipped with an opening rear fuselage swing tail. Nine KC-97s, surplus to USAF requirements, were purchased soon afterwards. These were to serve in the transport, in-flight refuelling and electronic warfare roles before being retired from service in April 1978. Details of the specific aircraft are:

Type	IAF No	Registration
Boeing B-377	96	4X-FPZ
	97	4X-FPY
	98	4X-FPX
	15	4X-FPW
	10	4X-FPV
Boeing KC-97F	38	4X-FPU
Boeing KC-97G	31	4X-FPT
	37	4X-FPS
	33	4X-FPR
	32	4X-FPQ
	30	4X-FPP
	35	4X-FPO
	39	4X-FPN
	40	4X-FPM

All of these types carried both IAF number and the 4X Civil Registration letters. Boeing B-377s operated in natural metal, with a white upper fuselage spine above a blue cheat line along the fuselage window positions, running from nose to tail.

Boeing KC-97s were painted in USAF Air Defence Gray, FS 16473, with white upper fuselage over a narrow blue cheat line, running under the cockpit windows then turning-up to run over the fuselage windows to the tail. Israeli KC-97s did not operate with outer wing jet pods.

Two new types of helicopter also entered IAF service during this period. In 1965, Israel purchased seven Agusta-Bell 47G-2s and six Bell 47Gs from

Uppersurface camouflage patterns
In 1955 the IAF standardised on a camouflage scheme of
Israeli produced paint, Blue and Brown uppersurfaces
with Light Grey undersides. A 'typical' pattern was
developed for both straight-wing and swept-wing aircraft.
However, it was not long before variations to the 'typical'
pattern appeared, including reverse patterns to the
standard and mirror schemes. The particular patterns
illustrated here are based on the Mystere IVA planform.

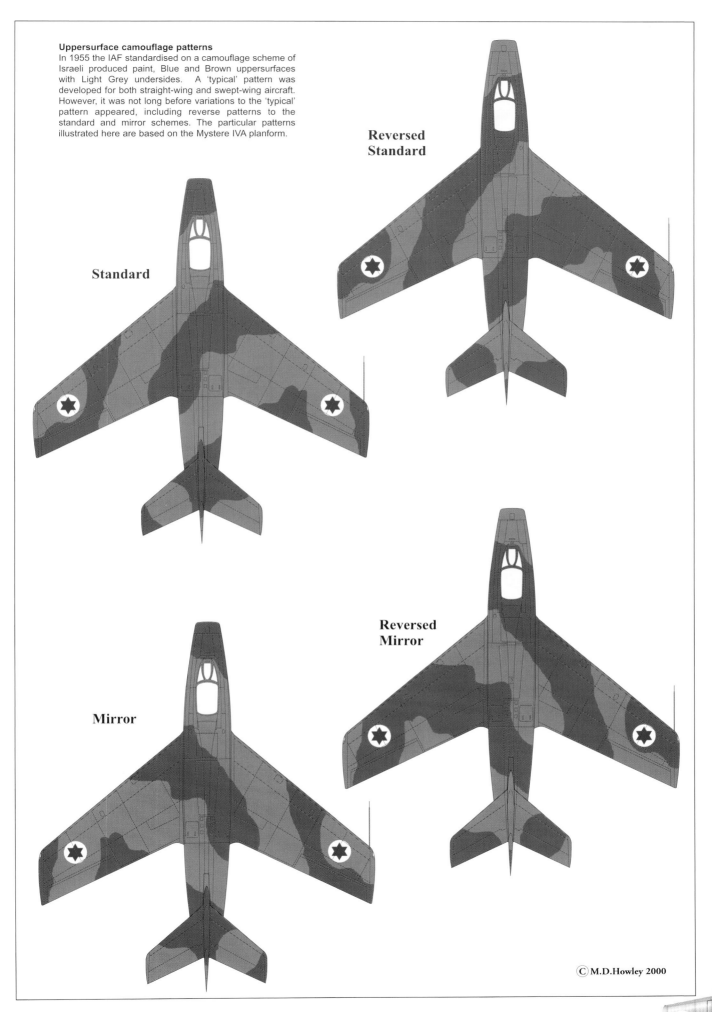

Reversed
Standard

Standard

Reversed
Mirror

Mirror

© M.D.Howley 2000

Above: Boeing B-377 Stratocruiser transports entered service with the IAF in July 1964, with the 'International' Squadron. Altogether five B-377 versions and nine KC-97 versions would enter service, the last being withdrawn in April 1978.

France. These thirteen aircraft were to serve as trainers and helped to convert fixed wing pilots on to helicopters. They also served in the liaison role. It is believed that they were painted in FS 34079 Green, similar to the Alouette, with red fuel tanks and tail boom stabiliser.

At the opposite end of the scale, Israel also bought from France twelve Sud Aviation SA-321K Super Frelon heavy transport and assault helicopters. The first four arrived in Israel in April 1966, with the rest following between late 1967 and early 1969. The Super Frelons were painted in France and delivered in an uppersurface camouflage pattern of Light Brown, (close to FS 33448) and Dark Green, (close to FS 34102). The undersides were painted Light Blue, (close to FS 35526). With these

Left: Super Frelons of the 'Heavy Lift' Squadron. Unlike other IAF types, these helicopters were painted in a Green and Brown upper surface camouflage with Light Blue undersides. Note the stencil information and Squadron badge on the tail boom.

Below: Members of the new 'Heavy Lift' Super Frelon Squadron parade in front of their new Squadron Colours. The IAF purchased twelve Sud Aviation 321K Super Frelons, the first arriving in Israel in April 1966. And yes, it does rain in Israel sometimes !

helicopters, Israel now had a long range heavy lift capacity, which it was to put into effect during the Six Day War and afterwards.

Completing the purchases from France, surplus Dassault Ouragans were acquired and, after refurbishment, equipped a second Squadron, the 'Lion's Head' as it was called then - the squadron is now known as 'Knights of the Orange Tail'.

The 'gift' of a MiG

Clashes between Israel and its Arab neighbours still erupted from time to time. As the teething problems with the Mirage began to be put right and the pilots gained experience, an effective fighting force began to emerge. However, they did receive help from an unexpected source to get the measure of the MiG-21. On 16 August 1966, following an Israeli Intelligence Operation, an Iraqi defector landed at Hatzor delivering to the IAF a brand new MiG-21. The IAF handed the aircraft over to the technicians at Israeli Aircraft Industries for a thorough investigation, and whilst there it was flown by test pilot Danny Shapira. The strengths and weaknesses of the MiG-21 were revealed and disseminated to the Squadrons. Mirage pilots also had the opportunity to practice 'dog-fights' with the MiG, now given Israeli Air Force markings and the serial number '007'. The next clash did not involve a MiG-21.

First missile 'kill'

On 13 November 1966, two Mirages from the 'Bat' Squadron, led by their commander, Major Ran Ronen, were ordered to intercept Jordanian Hawker Hunters detected over the Hebron area. Earlier that day Israeli ground forces, including tanks and artillery, had attacked Jordanian positions at Sammu south of Hebron, after three IDF soldiers were killed and six wounded whilst on patrol the previous day. The Hunters were scrambled to assist the defending Jordanians. When the aircraft met, a dog-

Below: '798' one of the two dedicated photo reconnaissance Mirage IIIRJs, delivered in March 1964, taking off on another mission.

fight began with the Jordanian pilots using the advantages of the Hunter at low altitude to the full. Ronen, flying Mirage IIICJ number '784' could not bring his guns to bear on the Hunter he tailed through the narrow valleys and it was only when it had to climb to avoid a hill that his shells struck home. The Jordanian pilot ejected from his stricken aircraft, but the angle of ejection was such that he hit the side of a hill and was killed.

Two weeks later on 29 November, two Mirages from 101 Squadron on patrol over the southern border with Egypt, were ordered to intercept two unidentified aircraft showing on radar. These turned out to be Egyptian MiG-19s, and Mirage pilot Captain Michael Haber, having gained a radar lock on one of the MiGs at a range of two kilometres, fired his Matra R-530 missile. This time the radar lock held, and the MiG exploded - a first for this missile and the first missile shoot-down for the IAF. The other MiG-19 was hit by gunfire from Haber's wingman, its pilot ejecting to safety.

Six - nil!

For several months, the Israel's northern border area had been subjected to guerrilla raids from Syria and Jordan and regular bombardment by Syrian artillery. On 7 April 1967, Syrian gun positions opened fire on Israeli farm tractors in an escalation of these attacks and, after a UN negotiated cease-fire was broken again by Syrian shell-fire, the IDF called in the Air Force to silence the Syrian guns. At 1.30pm Vautours and Mystère IVs from Ramat David bombed and strafed the Syrian artillery and tank positions. The action continued throughout the afternoon, and it was not long before Syrian MiGs were detected heading for the area.

Providing cover for the attacking aircraft, two 101 Squadron Mirages piloted by Captain Yiftah Spector and Captain Benny Romach, engaged four MiG-21s over the Syrian town of Kuneitra. The two Mirages chased the MiGs away almost to Damascus, before being able to close the range sufficiently for accurate gun fire. Both Mirages were able to claim a MiG destroyed.

At 4.00pm, Major Ezra 'Baban'

Dotan, leading a formation of 'Bat' Squadron Mirage IIICJs, engaged four MiG-21s. Dotan's *Shafrir* missile missed, but his gunfire accounted for a MiG which crashed near Kibbutz Shamir.

With Dotan from the 'Bat' Squadron were Major Ran Ronen and Captain Averham Shalmon. Ronen's *Shafrir* missile also missed his target, but his gunfire hit the fuselage drop-tank and the pilot ejected from the burning aircraft. Shalmon's target MiG-21 had luck on its side. Not only did two *Shafrir* missiles miss their target, the cannon hits only caused damage and it was able to escape back to its base.

Nearby, Captain Avi Laner of the 'First Jet' Squadron, flying Mirage IIICJ number '60', engaged a MiG-21 at a range of less than 200 metres. As his cannon shells struck, the MiG exploded in a huge fireball which he had to fly through, because he was so close. On emerging, his aircraft was covered in a black film which obscured his vision, and he had to be escorted back to base where on landing his aircraft became known as the 'Black Mirage'!

Finally, Captain Averham Slapek in a 101 Squadron Mirage IIICJ attacked two MiG-21s seen over the Yarmuk Valley between Syria and Jordan. Catching up with one of them, Slapek fired a long burst from his 30mm cannons and the MiG exploded. The day ended with the successful operation against the Syrian guns and the destruction of six MiG-21s, all without loss to the IAF.

The day was also a personal triumph for Air Force Commander Moti Hod who was promoted to Major General with immediate effect. He had succeeded Ezer Weizman on 27 April 1966 and continued the path of quality and professionalism. Like Ezer, he believed that the next war would only be won with the destruction of the enemy's air power, and that meant attacking their airfields in a swift 'knock-out' blow. A plan, given the name *'Moked'* (Hebrew for Focus), was developed and circulated to the Squadrons, each of which had a given role and targets. These roles were practiced over and over again. As predicted, the time did come for the plan to be put into action.

The Six Day War
The Path to War

The months prior to the Six Day War were characterised by increases in tension and conflict, especially terrorist guerrilla action against Israel. Following Israeli action in response to the Syrian shelling of its Northern settlements, in early May 1967, the USSR informed Egypt that Israel had mobilised troops in the North with the intention of attacking Syria. Israel denied this and invited the Russian Ambassador to the North to see for himself. Nevertheless, this was believed by the Arab nations, particularly after Israeli reprisal raids against Syria and Jordan and they prepared for war.

On the 16 May 1967, Egypt put her armed forces on a state of emergency,

and two days later President Nasser requested the withdrawal of United Nations Peace-keeping troops in Sinai. Further Egyptian troops then moved into Sinai, taking station at Sharm-El-Sheik and again, closing the Straits of Tiran to Israeli Shipping. An action which Israel had already stated could be a cause for war.

As Israel's Arab neighbours took a more belligerent stance, other nations rallied to support them as the proclamation of a *'Jihad'* or Holy War gained momentum. Algeria mobilised her troops and Morocco promised assistance in the event of Israeli aggression. However, it was King Hussein of Jordan

Heading: The man and the machine! Major General Itzhak Rabin, IDF Chief of Staff in 1967, in front of Mirage IIIC '745' of the 'First Jet' Squadron at Ramat David. Mirage '745' carries three kill markings - two Iraqi and one Lebanese. On the second day of the War, the Squadron Deputy Commander, Major Uri Even-Nir intercepted a flight of Lebanese Hawker Hunters and eventually shot one down. There were no further interventions by the Lebanese Air Force. The aircraft sports a red fuselage stripe, and as can be seen from the reflections, was highly polished.

Below: Dassault Mystère IVA '71' of the 'Flying Wing' Squadron landing using a tail chute for braking. Mystères from this unit attacked Fayid airfield in the opening hours of the War destroying many fighter aircraft including MiG-21s.

meeting President Nasser on 30 May that gave the Israelis real concern. Jordan joined the alliance with Egypt and Syria, placing her Troops under Egyptian command and allowing Egyptian Troops to operate from her territory. The following day, Iraqi Troops began to arrive in Jordan.

Parts of Israel in-between the Jordanian West Bank Territories and the Mediterranean Sea are less than 12 miles wide, and Israel feared being cut in two. As Arab rhetoric against Israel increased, with calls to drive the Jews into the sea, and the military build up gathered pace, time was against Israel. On 5 June 1967, Israel decided to pre-empt the Arab action and strike first, putting Operation 'Moked' into effect.

'Operation Moked'

The aim of 'Operation Moked' was the destruction of the Arab Air Forces before they could be massed and used against Israeli Forces and centres of population. It was an all embracing plan to deal with the Air Forces of Egypt, Jordan, Syria, Lebanon and Iraq. Egypt, because of her proximity to Israel and the size of her Air Force, was deemed the greatest threat and scheduled for the first waves of attack.

Each Israeli Air Force Squadron had its own unique part to play. Their aircraft were grouped into formations of four aircraft, each formation having a specific target list for each phase of the Operation. This was normally a target to bomb, such as a runway, or group of buildings, followed by a number of strafing runs on parked aircraft and airfield targets of opportunity. All this had to be achieved at specific times for maximum effect and to avoid disrupting

Below: Sud Vautour IIA '12' of the 'Knights of the North' Squadron landing at Ramat David. Vautours took part in the attack on Cairo West airfield, home to a squadron of Tupolev Tu-16 Bombers. Their four 30mm DEFA cannons proved very effective in the destruction of these large bombers.

Israeli Air Force Order of Battle at the start of the Six Day War

Squadron	Aircraft	Location
Front Line Fighters		
101 Squadron	Mirage IIICJ	Hatzor
'First Jet' Squadron	Mirage IIICJ	Ramat David
The 'Bat' Squadron	Mirage IIICJ	Tel Nof
The 'Scorpions'	Super Mystère B2	Hatzor
The 'Valley' Squadron	Mystère IV	Ramat David
The 'Flying Wing' Squadron	Mystère IV	Tel Nof
The 'Hornet' Squadron	Ouragan	Hatzor
The 'Lion's Head' Squadron	Ouragan	Ramat David
The 'Knights of the North'	Vautour II	Ramat David
Armed Trainers		
The Flying School	Fouga Magister	Hatzerim
Light Aircraft and Liaison		
The 'Flying Camel' Squadron	Mixed types: Piper Cub and Dornier 27	Various Locations HQ Sde Dov
Transports		
The 'Elephant' Squadron	Nord Noratlas	Lod
The 'International' Squadron	Dakota/Stratocruiser	Lod
Helicopters		
The 'Super Frelon' Squadron	Super Frelon	Tel Nof
The 'Rolling Swords' Squadron	Sikorsky S-58	Tel Nof
The 'Southern Bells' Squadron	Bell 47/Alouette II	Tel Nof

other attacking formations and the impetus of the Operation.

Each target was carefully selected, as were the aircraft allocated to attack. Egyptian Air Bases in Sinai were allocated to Ouragan and armed Fouga Magister Squadrons because of the limited range of these aircraft. The more distant Arab airfields were allocated to the Vautours. However, all plans are subject to change, and Mirage IIICJs were also allocated to support the Ouragans and Magisters when Egyptian MiG-21s were sent into Sinai by President Nasser.

Early morning on Monday 5 June 1967, and throughout Israel airfields reverberated to the sound of heavily laden aircraft taking-off and heading out to sea. When the Israeli aircraft reached their designated turning points, they changed course and headed inland to their airfield targets. The attacks were timed to strike ten key Egyptian airfields simultaneously at 08.45am local time.

The first attacks were the Sinai airfields at El Arish, Bir Gifgafa, Jebel Libni and Bir Thamada. These were the closest to Israel and would also pose a

threat to IDF ground forces, preparing to mount an assault into Sinai. The air attacks also hit the Suez Canal Zone airfields of Abu Sueir, Inchas, Fayid and Kabrit. These were large airfields close to Sinai, and all home to regiments of MiG-21s, the major threat to IAF air activity. Also included in these first attacks were the airfields at Cairo West and Beni Sueif. These were the home bases of Egypt's Tupolev Tu-16 bombers, which could cause major damage to Israel's towns and cities. An eleventh airfield, Cairo International Airport, was also hit in this opening attack, when the Mirages tasked to bomb Inchas airfield were prevented from doing so by fog, and attacked military aircraft they spotted at Cairo International instead.

Each airfield would be hit by formations of attacking aircraft who would then return to their home base to re-fuel and re-arm before being sent back as another attacking formation. From landing to take-off, turnaround times of less than ten minutes were achieved, a testimony to the IAF ground staff who had practiced long and hard to reach these times, not then matched by any other air force. Depending on the airfield attacked, it was possible for Israeli pilots to be back over their targets within thirty minutes to an hour of their previous attack, and other formations would have hit the targets in between these times. The raids on these first airfields lasted

Above: Dassault Ouragan '68' of the 'Hornet' Squadron. Ouragans attacked the Sinai airfields on the opening day, with the 'Hornets' hitting Bir Gifgafa and the 'Lion's Head' hitting El Arish. Strike damage had to be confined to aircraft targets as the IAF wanted to use the airfields to support their ground advance.

Below: Dassault Super Mystère B2 '31' of the 'Scorpion' Squadron. These aircraft were the first to hit Kabrit Airfield in the Canal Zone destroying many Egyptian MiG-17s. Having refuelled and re-armed they were then back in action over Inchas airfield.

eighty minutes and the effect on the Egyptian Air Force was devastating.

In those eighty minutes, one hundred and ninety-seven Egyptian aircraft, including all their Tu-16s had been destroyed - one hundred and eighty-nine on the ground and eight MiG-21s in the air. Six of the airfields were totally inoperable and the others were severely damaged. Additionally, sixteen radar stations had been destroyed.

The IAF had allocated one hundred and eighty-five aircraft to these attacks, losing nine by the end of the day, following repeat attacks and further attacks against other Egyptian airfields

Below: Dassault Ouragan '69' of the 'Hornet' Squadron. The two Ouragan units provided close support for Israeli troops advancing across Sinai and took a heavy toll of Egyptian vehicles when they were caught in the narrow confines of the Mitla Pass.

later that morning and early in the afternoon.

The time of 8.45am Egyptian Time, chosen for these attacks was carefully planned:-
• It was the practice of the Egyptian Air Force to go on high alert each day at dawn, putting interceptor MiG-21s on stand-by and mounting air patrols against any potential threat. By 8.45am, these patrols would have returned to base and the alert lessened, thus their guard would be lowered.
• The Egyptian Air Force was a very regimented Force, with command and control in the hands of Senior Officers, many who lived off base with their families. The IAF knew that it was normal for these Officers to work a 'nine 'til five' day, so by striking at 8.45am, these Officers would be on their journeys to work. Their absence from the Base would

Above: A Mirage IIICJ of the 'First Jet' Squadron re-arming and refuelling at Ramat David. This Squadron flew many air defence missions over the North of Israel, shooting down Syrian, Jordanian and one Lebanese aircraft - note the five 'kill' marks beneath the cockpit which appear to be four Syrian and one Jordanian - and the highly polished natural metal finish.

add to confusion and lack of action.
• Early June is characterised by dense early morning mists over the Nile Delta, Upper Suez, North Sinai Coast and the Bitter Lakes. These mists usually disperse by 8.00am leaving clear and still, early morning conditions, ideal for bombing missions.

The IAF achieved complete surprise. The first attacking formations met very little resistance. However, as the day progressed, resistance increased, but by then, the damage had been done.

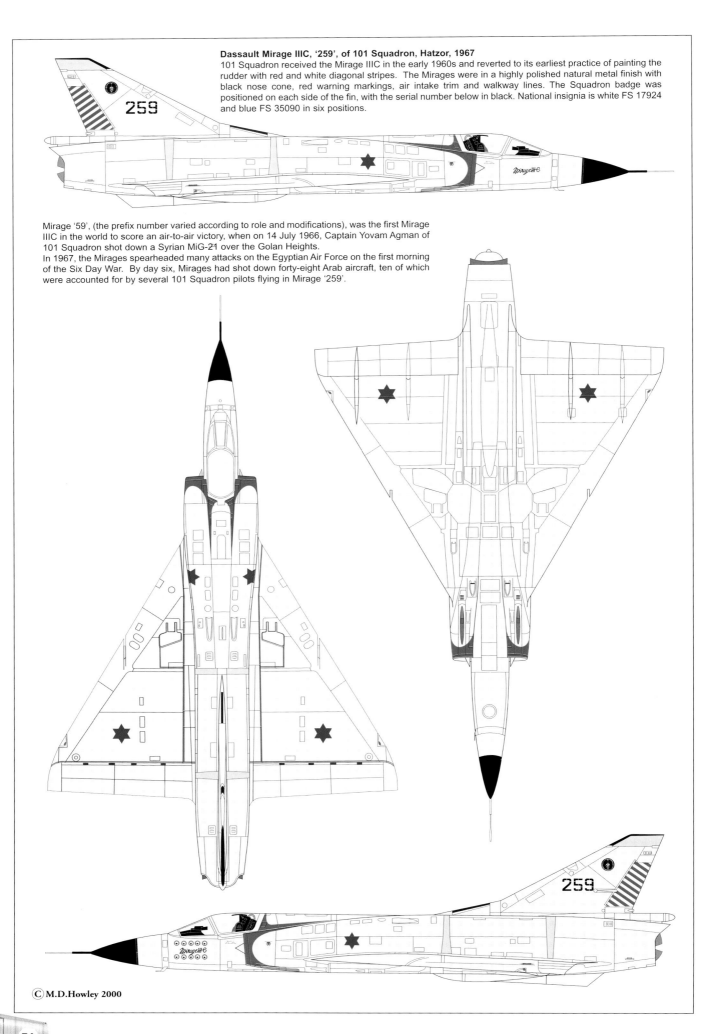

Dassault Mirage IIIC, '259', of 101 Squadron, Hatzor, 1967
101 Squadron received the Mirage IIIC in the early 1960s and reverted to its earliest practice of painting the rudder with red and white diagonal stripes. The Mirages were in a highly polished natural metal finish with black nose cone, red warning markings, air intake trim and walkway lines. The Squadron badge was positioned on each side of the fin, with the serial number below in black. National insignia is white FS 17924 and blue FS 35090 in six positions.

Mirage '59', (the prefix number varied according to role and modifications), was the first Mirage IIIC in the world to score an air-to-air victory, when on 14 July 1966, Captain Yovam Agman of 101 Squadron shot down a Syrian MiG-21 over the Golan Heights.
In 1967, the Mirages spearheaded many attacks on the Egyptian Air Force on the first morning of the Six Day War. By day six, Mirages had shot down forty-eight Arab aircraft, ten of which were accounted for by several 101 Squadron pilots flying in Mirage '259'.

© M.D.Howley 2000

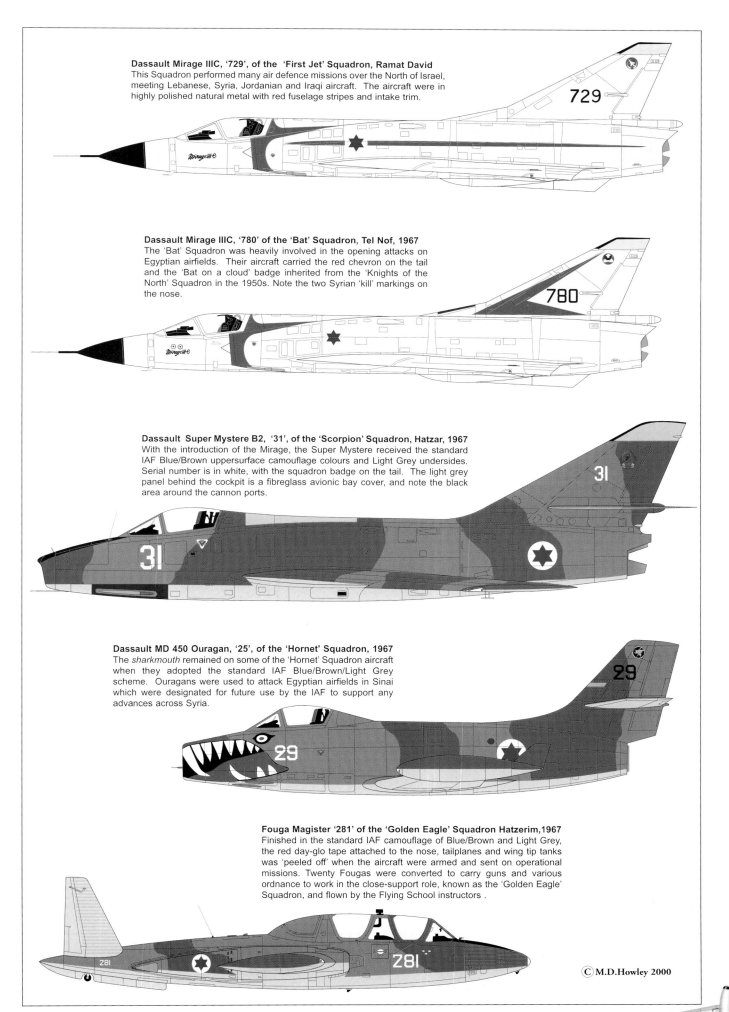

Dassault Mirage IIIC, '729', of the 'First Jet' Squadron, Ramat David
This Squadron performed many air defence missions over the North of Israel, meeting Lebanese, Syria, Jordanian and Iraqi aircraft. The aircraft were in highly polished natural metal with red fuselage stripes and intake trim.

Dassault Mirage IIIC, '780' of the 'Bat' Squadron, Tel Nof, 1967
The 'Bat' Squadron was heavily involved in the opening attacks on Egyptian airfields. Their aircraft carried the red chevron on the tail and the 'Bat on a cloud' badge inherited from the 'Knights of the North' Squadron in the 1950s. Note the two Syrian 'kill' markings on the nose.

Dassault Super Mystere B2, '31', of the 'Scorpion' Squadron, Hatzar, 1967
With the introduction of the Mirage, the Super Mystere received the standard IAF Blue/Brown uppersurface camouflage colours and Light Grey undersides. Serial number is in white, with the squadron badge on the tail. The light grey panel behind the cockpit is a fibreglass avionic bay cover, and note the black area around the cannon ports.

Dassault MD 450 Ouragan, '25', of the 'Hornet' Squadron, 1967
The *sharkmouth* remained on some of the 'Hornet' Squadron aircraft when they adopted the standard IAF Blue/Brown/Light Grey scheme. Ouragans were used to attack Egyptian airfields in Sinai which were designated for future use by the IAF to support any advances across Syria.

Fouga Magister '281' of the 'Golden Eagle' Squadron Hatzerim,1967
Finished in the standard IAF camouflage of Blue/Brown and Light Grey, the red day-glo tape attached to the nose, tailplanes and wing tip tanks was 'peeled off' when the aircraft were armed and sent on operational missions. Twenty Fougas were converted to carry guns and various ordnance to work in the close-support role, known as the 'Golden Eagle' Squadron, and flown by the Flying School instructors.

© M.D.Howley 2000

Fayid Airfield in the Canal Zone was attacked by Mystère IVs of the 'Flying Wing' Squadron, in four Flights of four aircraft, each ten minutes apart. The first flight, led by Future Air Force Commander Avihu Ben-Nun, arrived over Fayid at the designated time and proceeded to drop their bombs on the runway at one-third and two-thirds along its length. Free of their bombs, the Mystères then attacked the aircraft on the ground, Ben-Nun hitting two MiG-21s approaching the runway to take off.

Flying around the airfield, Ben-Nun spotted an Antonov An 12 landing on the runway amongst the explosions. However, their orders were to destroy the MiGs so the transport was left unharmed. By the time his formation left Fayid, sixteen of the forty MiGs sighted were destroyed and the runway had been badly damaged. The other, following formations, would destroy many more MiGs and put the runway completely out of action. It was later discovered that the Antonov was carrying the Egyptian Chief of Staff and several other Senior Officers who were returning after a visit to troops in Sinai. The Antonov's Captain was decorated for his skill, making a safe landing under heavy fire.

Later, the IAF returned to Egyptian skies to attack fourteen airfields including several others that had not been on the 'initial target' list. These were Mansura, Helwan, Almaza, El-Minya, Bilbis, Luxor, and in the south, the Red Sea airfields at Hurghada and Ras Banas. Cairo International, Egypt's main civil airport was not originally scheduled for attack, but as surviving aircraft from the first raids began to congregate there because their own bases' runways were still operable, this airfield was also added to the list.

Forewarned from the earlier raids, these airfields put up spirited defences and more MiGs were encountered in the air. By now, the IAF Squadrons were on their fourth or fifth missions of the day.

The 'Bat' Squadron from Tel Nof was having a very busy time. Flights of four aircraft from this Squadron carried out the first attack on Inchas, bombing the runway and shooting at any MiGs they could find. Other Flights formed the second attacking formation, hitting Cairo West, which had been on the receiving end of a 'Knights of the North' Vautour attack minutes earlier. Here the Mirage IIICJs, further damaged the runways, and attacked the Tu-16 bombers dispersed throughout the field. In their natural metal finishes, the Israeli pilots easily spotted them gleaming in the sun. The four 30mm cannons in the nose of the Vautour had made short work of destroying many of these bombers, but the Mirages found five more and left them in flames.

Meanwhile, the Mirage IIICJs that had attacked Inchas were refuelled, rearmed and then sent to attack Abu Sueir in the Canal Zone. This airfield was the home to Il-28 'Beagle' bombers and the Mirages caused more damage to the airfield and destroyed a further ten Il-28s, before heading home.

Their next raid was against Hurghada on the Red Sea, just south of Sharm-El-Sheikh. Over the preceding months, the IAF had increased its air activity over the Red Sea and the Gulf of Aqaba. The Egyptians, fearing an attack from the south, moved a Squadron of MiG-21s to Hurghada to counter this threat. As the Mirages approached, they were met by heavy anti-aircraft fire, but they pressed on with the attack, hitting the runway with their bombs and putting it out of action.

Re-grouping away from the airfield to avoid the 'flak', the Mirages turned to begin their ground strafing runs, where they succeeded in destroying more MiGs and a Mil 8 helicopter. During these runs, the formation was attacked by four MiG-19s. In the brief dogfight that followed, three of the MiGs were shot down, two by the formation leader Ran Ronen. The remaining MiG-19 was destroyed when it landed on Hurghada's runway and crashed into a bomb crater.

Equally busy that morning were the Super Mystère B2s of the 'Scorpion' Squadron based at Hatzor. The first target for some of their formations was the Canal Zone airfield at Kabrit, were they bombed the runway and destroyed several of the resident MiG-17s. After a quick turnaround, the Super Mystères were back over Egypt as part of the second wave, attacking Inchas, (following close behind the 'Bat' Squadron mentioned previously). By now, Inchas was on full alert and the Super Mystères had to take avoiding action when SAM-2 missiles were fired. Again the runway

Right: A close-up of the nose of Dassault Mirage IIICJ '259' of 101 Squadron shown at the bottom of the opposite page. In Day One of the War, IAF Mirages of all three Mirage-equipped units were heavily engaged in action over Syria, where five airfields were attacked.

was bombed and several more MiGs destroyed by cannon fire.

Later in the morning, formations of the Super Mystère B2s were also tasked to bomb Mansura airfield in the Nile Delta region. However, the Mirages could not locate the airfield and were re-directed to hit Egyptian military positions in Sinai. An attacking formation following the Super Mystères also failed to find the airfield. However, the third attacking formation struck lucky, when they spotted a MiG on a landing approach to the field and followed it down to attack.

Over Sinai, it was the Ouragan Squadrons that were tasked to deal with the Egyptian Airfields. Whilst the 'Hornet' Squadron attacked Bir Gifgafa, the Ouragans of the 'Lion Head' Squadron struck at El Arish. Unlike all the other raids, the runways at El Arish were not bombed, as the IAF had plans to operate from this airfield, using it as a forward air base to support its ground operations.

The later attacks on Egyptian Airfields accounted for a further one hundred and seven aircraft, making the morning's total three hundred and four aircraft destroyed and nineteen airfields put out of action. However, early afternoon also saw intervention by Jordanian and Syrian aircraft so the IAF threw its weight to the north and east.

Syria, Jordan and Iraq

Late in the morning of 5 June 1967, Ramat David came under fire from Jordanian artillery. Little damage was done but the base was put on full alert. In the afternoon, Syrian MiG-21s were spotted entering Israeli airspace over the Sea of Galilee. Three attacked the airfield at Mahanayim, whilst others attacked a Kibbutz and a water pumping station. More serious was an attack by sixteen Jordanian Hawker Hunters which struck at the Israeli coastal resort of Netanya and the airfield at Kfir Sirkin, where a Nord Noratlas was destroyed. Mirage IIICJs from the 'Bat' Squadron at Tel Nof were scrambled to intercept, and chased the Hunters back over the River Jordan to Amman, where one was shot down.

Shortly afterwards, the IAF dispatched raids to the Jordanian airfields at Amman and Mafraq, putting both out of action and destroying twenty-one of the twenty-four Hunters in Jordanian service! Amman was hit by formations of Mystère IVs which bombed the runways first, then strafed ground targets including Alouette helicopters and a line up of three De Havilland Doves, one belonging to the British Air Attaché. In less than thirty minutes, the Jordanian Air Force ceased to exist, and surviving pilots were sent to Iraq.

Raids were also dispatched to Syria, attacking airfields at Damascus, Maj Riyal, Dumayr, Seikel and T4 (named after its position on an Oil pipeline).

Once again, the 'Scorpion' Super Mystère B2 formations were amongst the first into action. At Dumayr, the Israelis

were surprised to find that the Syrians had not 'closed the base' for action. Cairo Radio was reporting that the Egyptian Air Force was bombing Israeli airfields, and whether the Syrians were taken in by this or not, Syrian MiGs were lined up in neat rows in the open, with no attempt made at dispersal or camouflage. The Israeli jets bombed the runways and then 'set about' the parked MiGs.

The Commander of the 'Scorpion' Squadron, Yalo Shavit, was leading a formation in an attack on Seikel, when following their bomb run, they spotted two MiG-21s diving on them from behind. Yalo called his formation to begin evasive manoeuvres and they split into pairs, but the MiGs stuck with them and a dogfight began with each side trying to get the other into a 'shoot-down' position. Yalo succeeded in getting on the tail of the first MiG-21 and fired a long burst, sending it crashing on the airfield. His formation Number Two, hit the second MiG, shooting off a wing.

The Mirages of the 'Bat' Squadron were tasked to attack the Syrian Airfield at T4. This is an area in open country in the north of Syria - T4 actually being a pumping station on the Kirkuk to Tripoli Oil Pipeline, giving its 'name' to this location. The airfield was quite large and by mid-afternoon, housed many aircraft that had escaped the earlier attacks on the other Syrian Airfields. Here the Syrians were better prepared and the anti-aircraft fire was particularly heavy. The Mirages also came under attack by MiG-21s, and succeeded in shooting

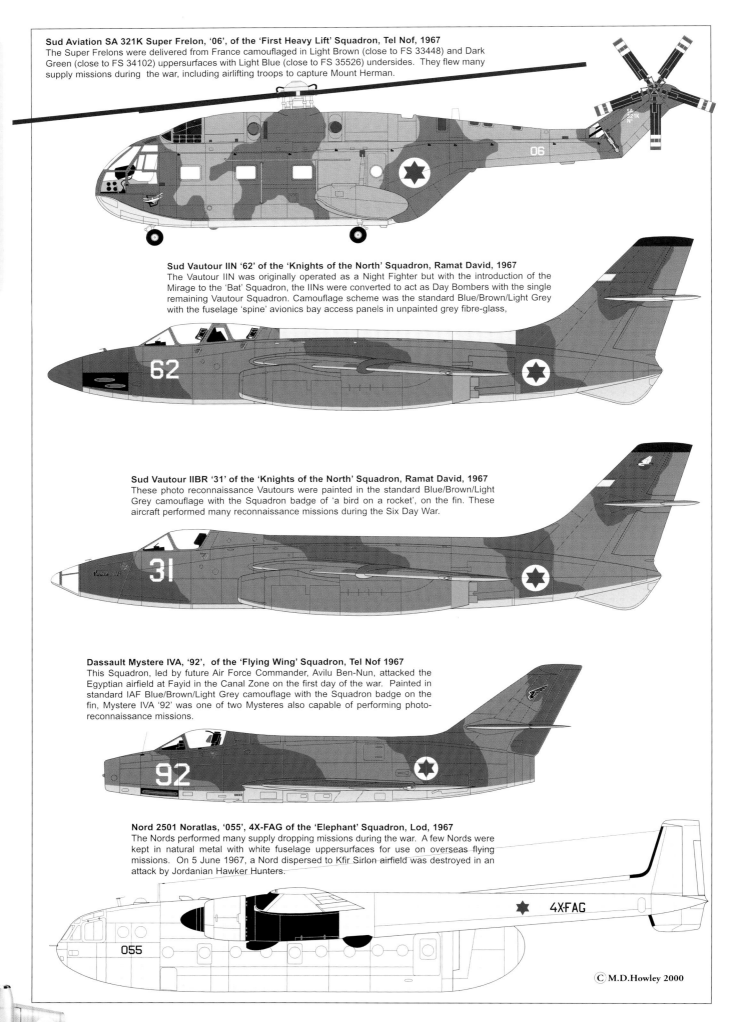

Sud Aviation SA 321K Super Frelon, '06', of the 'First Heavy Lift' Squadron, Tel Nof, 1967
The Super Frelons were delivered from France camouflaged in Light Brown (close to FS 33448) and Dark Green (close to FS 34102) uppersurfaces with Light Blue (close to FS 35526) undersides. They flew many supply missions during the war, including airlifting troops to capture Mount Herman.

Sud Vautour IIN '62' of the 'Knights of the North' Squadron, Ramat David, 1967
The Vautour IIN was originally operated as a Night Fighter but with the introduction of the Mirage to the 'Bat' Squadron, the IINs were converted to act as Day Bombers with the single remaining Vautour Squadron. Camouflage scheme was the standard Blue/Brown/Light Grey with the fuselage 'spine' avionics bay access panels in unpainted grey fibre-glass,

Sud Vautour IIBR '31' of the 'Knights of the North' Squadron, Ramat David, 1967
These photo reconnaissance Vautours were painted in the standard Blue/Brown/Light Grey camouflage with the Squadron badge of 'a bird on a rocket', on the fin. These aircraft performed many reconnaissance missions during the Six Day War.

Dassault Mystere IVA, '92', of the 'Flying Wing' Squadron, Tel Nof 1967
This Squadron, led by future Air Force Commander, Avilu Ben-Nun, attacked the Egyptian airfield at Fayid in the Canal Zone on the first day of the war. Painted in standard IAF Blue/Brown/Light Grey camouflage with the Squadron badge on the fin, Mystere IVA '92' was one of two Mysteres also capable of performing photo-reconnaissance missions.

Nord 2501 Noratlas, '055', 4X-FAG of the 'Elephant' Squadron, Lod, 1967
The Nords performed many supply dropping missions during the war. A few Nords were kept in natural metal with white fuselage uppersurfaces for use on overseas flying missions. On 5 June 1967, a Nord dispersed to Kfir Sirlon airfield was destroyed in an attack by Jordanian Hawker Hunters.

© M.D.Howley 2000

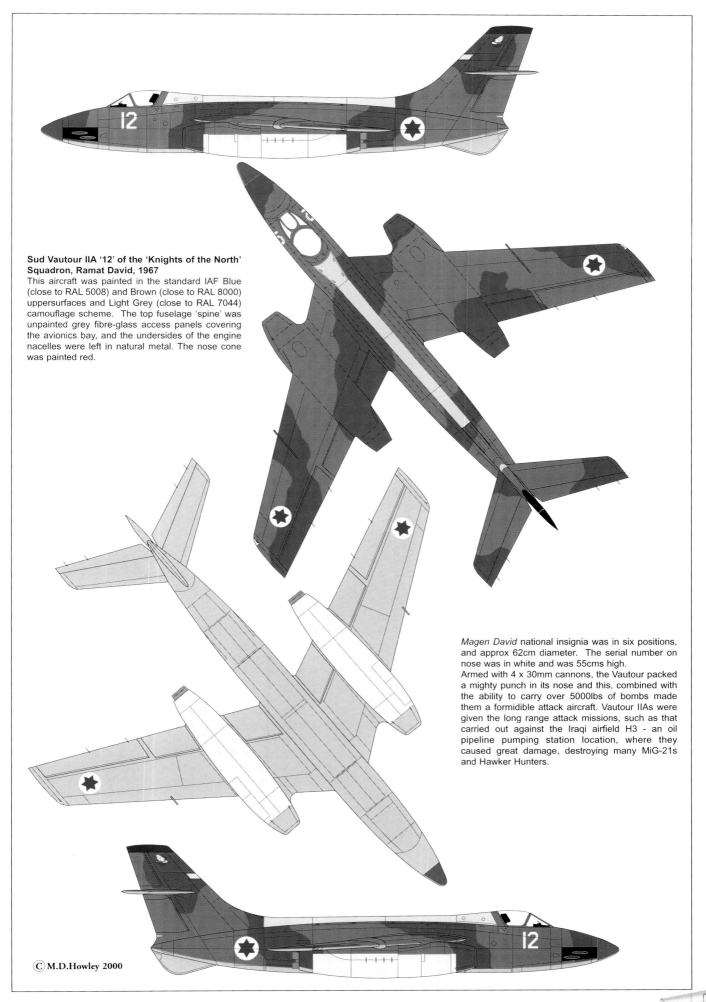

Sud Vautour IIA '12' of the 'Knights of the North' Squadron, Ramat David, 1967
This aircraft was painted in the standard IAF Blue (close to RAL 5008) and Brown (close to RAL 8000) uppersurfaces and Light Grey (close to RAL 7044) camouflage scheme. The top fuselage 'spine' was unpainted grey fibre-glass access panels covering the avionics bay, and the undersides of the engine nacelles were left in natural metal. The nose cone was painted red.

Magen David national insignia was in six positions, and approx 62cm diameter. The serial number on nose was in white and was 55cms high.
Armed with 4 x 30mm cannons, the Vautour packed a mighty punch in its nose and this, combined with the ability to carry over 5000lbs of bombs made them a formidible attack aircraft. Vautour IIAs were given the long range attack missions, such as that carried out against the Iraqi airfield H3 - an oil pipeline pumping station location, where they caused great damage, destroying many MiG-21s and Hawker Hunters.

© M.D.Howley 2000

Above: Fouga Magister '231' of the IAF Flying School photographed immediately prior to the Six Day War. Recognising their ground-attack potential, many Flying School Fougas were fitted with machine guns and rockets to offer close support to the ground troops. These aircraft had standard IAF Blue/Brown/Light Grey camouflage with red day-glo tape applied to their noses, tails and wingtips.

down two of them before disengaging from the attack.

The attacks on the Syrian Airfields destroyed fifty-three aircraft and caused severe damage to runways and airfield installations. Ten Israeli aircraft were lost. At the end of the first day, all effective air opposition against Israel had been crushed.

On Tuesday 6 June 1967, Day Two of the War, the residents of Netanya were again disturbed when three bombs exploded in a local factory. A large Tupolev Tu-16 bomber in Iraqi makings was spotted at low level above the town, turning north, away from the scene. The bomber's flight path took it over Ramat David where it was engaged by the airfield defence units and hit several times. A patrolling Mirage IIICJ that had been called to intercept, spotted the damaged bomber over nearby Megiddo and promptly shot it down. Tragically, it

crashed into a Military Camp and several soldiers were killed.

To prevent further raids by Iraq, the Air Force dispatched a formation of Vautour IIs, escorted by Mirage IIICJs to the Iraqi Airfield at H3, another location on the same Pipeline as the Syrian Base at T4. The attack on H3 was not going to be easy. The Iraqis were well prepared and with the benefit of additional Jordanian Hunter pilots, were able to maintain constant air patrols. Sure enough, as the formations approached, MiG-21s were scrambled into the air to challenge them, and Iraqi Hunters already airborne, dived onto the Israeli formations. Sticking strictly to the mission objectives, the Vautours bombed the runway and strafed parked aircraft, leaving the Mirages to defend them.

However, coming out of one pass, a Vautour pilot found a Hunter directly in front and opened fire with his four 30mm cannons The Hunter broke apart, falling into the airfield below. The Vautours eventually peeled away from the airfield and its dense anti-aircraft fire, leaving MiG-21s, Hawker Hunters and Il-14 transports in flames. The raid had cost the Israelis three aircraft destroyed.

From now on, the IAF would concentrate on supporting Israel's ground

forces and the air defence of the state.

Day Two also brought a brief intervention by the Lebanon, when Hawker Hunters were detected over northern Israel and the Mirages of the 'First Jet' Squadron, scrambled to intercept. The leader of the Alert Flight, Uri Even-Nir, flying Mirage IIICJ '745', was guided to the Lebanese border where he was given permission to pursue a target spotted leaving Israeli air space. He soon caught up and identified the target as a single Hunter, which he brought down after several bursts of fire, near the Airfield at Riyaq, east of Beirut. Lebanon played no further part in the War.

Ground Support Operations

In addition to participating in 'Operation Moked', the IAF was also operating in support of the Israeli Army, which began offensive moves against the Egyptians into Sinai at 8.15am on Monday 5 June

Below: Fouga Magisters '220' and '209'. For the ground-attack role some twenty Flying School Magisters were converted to carry two machine guns in the nose and rockets under the wings as shown by these two examples. Note that the red day-glo 'trainer' tape has been removed from both these aircraft, leaving adhesive marks on the paintwork.

Above: Sud Aviation Super Frelon '09' of the 'Heavy Lift' Squadron. On the last day of the War, S-58s and the Super Frelons transported Israeli troops behind Syrian positions on Mount Hermon, enabling them to capture this strategically important position.

1967. Later that morning when news of the actions against Egypt were known, Jordanian Forces commenced action against Israel, shelling Ramat David, IDF positions near the West Bank and Jerusalem, and later, Tel Aviv. In response, the Israeli Army Central Command mounted a two-pronged assault towards Jerusalem starting at 2.25pm that afternoon.

Three years earlier, anticipating a need for close support aircraft, the IAF learned from its use of the Harvard, in previous actions that the solution could be armed training aircraft. Consequently, the IAF evaluated the Fouga Magister and found it to be ideal in this role - but did have reservations about its vulnerability over a modern battlefield. Twenty

Magisters were converted to carry two 7.62mm machine guns in the nose and were fitted with wing racks which could carry six 80mm air-to-ground rockets, in two groups of three under each wing, or a rack to hold a single 50kg bomb under each wing. In times of emergency, it was planned that these armed Magisters would be flown by the Flight School Instructors.

During the Six Day War, they were to prove their value time after time, starting with Day One. The Magisters were painted in the standard camouflage colours of Dark Blue and Brown uppersurfaces with Light Grey lower surfaces. As training aircraft, their nose, tail unit and wing tips were covered with strips of Fluorescent Red tape, stuck over the paintwork. For the offensive operations, these strips of tape were simply peeled off. It did leave lines of adhesive on the paintwork and looked messy, but appearance was the least of their concerns.

The IDF opened its Sinai assault with actions against Egyptian positions in Gaza, Khan Yunis and Rafah. Fouga Magisters attacked strongpoints and tank formations, clearing the way for the advancing troops. In the central part of Sinai, the Magisters hit Egyptian positions around El Arish, causing mayhem amongst the defenders when their rockets hit an Egyptian munitions train.

On the Jerusalem front, the IDF Central Command had its work cut out with limited forces in Jerusalem. It faced a hard slog against the Arab Legion to get there, before the Jordanian Army could reinforce its Jerusalem Garrison and overrun the small Israeli enclave. Already, an Armoured Column had crossed the River Jordan and was on the Jericho to Jerusalem road. It would not make Jerusalem.

Late in the afternoon as the Column entered a stretch of mountainside road, the Magisters sprung their ambush, hitting the lead and rear tanks, then spreading destruction as the remaining tanks and vehicles had no room for manoeuvre. Action against the Jordanian Army lasted well into the night, with Vautours attacking artillery positions and the Magisters hitting strongpoints, illuminated by search-lights on the roof of the Israeli Trades' Union Federation Building, the Histradrut, in Jerusalem!

Day Two continued with the Israeli advances into Sinai and towards Jerusalem. In Sinai, Mystère IVs attacked Egyptian Tank formations at Bir

Left: Sud Aviation Super Frelon '06' of the 'Heavy Lift' Squadron flying over the Sea of Galilee, with the Golan Heights in the background. This particular example of the Frelon sports the stabilising floats on the rear undercarriage legs.

Lahfan, as Ouragans and Magisters again worked as close-support to the advancing Units. IAF helicopters transported troops to Attack Points at Abu Agheila to the rear of the Egyptian defenders, and flew out the wounded and injured to hospitals in Israel.

During the afternoon, survivors from the Egyptian Air Force put in an appearance with two MiG-21s flying over Bir Lahfan and two Sukhoi Su-7s spotted over El Arish. All four aircraft were shot down by standing Mirage IIICJ patrols.

On the Jordan Front, Magisters hit Jordanian Patton tanks near Qulqilya and attacked an Iraqi Mechanised Brigade approaching the River Jordan near Damiya. Other aircraft joined in this attack, putting the Brigade out of action. That night, the attacks continued, but after two days of continuous action the

IAF took stock of its losses. By the end of Day Two, the IAF had now lost twenty-six aircraft:- seven Mystère IVs, five Ouragans, four Super Mystère B2s, two Mirage IIICJs, one Vautour II and seven Fouga Magisters.

Day Three saw the Egyptians and Jordanians in retreat. Having overrun the Egyptian first lines of defences and captured El Arish airfield, the Egyptian Forces withdrew to the Gidi and Mitla Passes in a general retreat from Sinai. At the Passes, the IAF bombed the leading vehicles and proceeded to annihilate the blocked columns leaving mile after mile of burned-out and destroyed tanks and other military vehicles. At other places, the Egyptians mounted blocking actions against the advancing Israeli tanks. One such action saw a depleted Israeli tank unit

Above: Super Frelon '10' shows the typical IAF standard Blue/Brown uppersurface camouflage pattern and the Light Grey undersides of the 'boat' hull. This aircraft does not have the amphibious capability, lacking the side stabilising floats on the rear undercarriage.

Below: Sikorsky S-58 '27' of the 'Rolling Sword' Squadron. Number 27 was from a batch of twenty-four acquired from West Germany. These *ex-Luftwaffe* helicopters were painted in RAL 6014 Olive Green overall, and rather than paint them in the full Blue/Brown Scheme, the IAF simply overpainted the German stencils and markings with the standard IAF Brown paint, so giving a disruptive RAL Olive Green/IAF Brown camouflage!

stumbling into a defensive position of twenty-eight Egyptian T-54 tanks. Air support in the form of attacking Ouragans saved the day for the Israeli tankers. The Egyptian Air force continued to mount sorties over Sinai, assisted by aircraft from Algeria. A MiG-21 and an Il-28 bomber were lost to Mirage patrols.

The end of the day brought jubilation for the Israelis as they had succeeded in capturing the Old City of Jerusalem, including the Holy Western Wall, lost to them in 1948. Fighting still continued throughout the West Bank as the Jordanians retreated to the River Jordan, with Ouragans and Magisters continuing to provide the 'aerial artillery'.

Days Four to Six
Day Four was taken up with Israeli Forces on the Banks of the Suez Canal and consolidating their positions in Sinai. At the tip of Sinai, Sharm-El-Sheikh was found to have been abandoned by the Egyptians and the airfield left intact. IAF Nord Noratlas transports, Dakotas and Stratocruisers all began to use the airfield, ferrying essential equipment and stores. Egyptian air sorties continued but their losses also continued to mount.

Day Five was dominated by an

Below: Nord Noratlas Transport, FX-FAP, of the 'Elephant' Squadron. The Nords flew countless supply missions and when the Israeli Army had captured Sharm El Sheikh airfield on the very southern tip of Sinai, they were able to ferry supplies and vital equipment right to the Front Line.

assault by the Israeli Army Northern Command against Syria along the Golan Heights. The Syrians had been pressing Northern Command since Day Two, when they sent a column of ten Tanks towards Kibbutz Dan, which were beaten back. Artillery fire from the Golan Heights had been incessant, and now the IDF was to stop any further Syrian action from the Heights once and for all. The Golan Heights dominate the landscape, running from the southern end of the Sea of Galilee for a distance of 60 kilometres to Mount Hermon in the north, giving the Syrians a commanding view over region.

Any Israeli advance would have to scale the Heights which were heavily defended by gun emplacements, tank traps and minefields. Again, using the IAF as aerial artillery, each advance was preceded by air attacks and artillery fire, and the IDF began to make headway up onto the Heights to tackle the Syrians head-on in a slogging match that was to last the next twenty-seven hours.

Time and again, the upper hand fell to the Israelis when their air power shifted the balance of battle. At Kala'a, a strategically important village, a desperate call for air support was seemingly answered when three Magisters appeared. However, the opposing tanks were so close together, that the aircraft could not tell them apart in the fading light. Realising the problem, the Israelis lit flares to mark their positions and the Magisters, now recognising the Syrians, delivered a

Above: As the Israeli Forces advanced across Sinai, supplies were airlifted in and the wounded evacuated out. Here, an IAF Douglas Dakota, and Nord Noratlas are seen on the re-supply effort. The smaller Dornier Do 27 of the 'Flying Camel' Squadron was used as a communications and liaison aircraft.

devastating attack.

At the last stage of this operation, Israeli troops were transported by Super Frelon and S-58 helicopters to Syrian rear positions and on to Mount Hermon. By mid-day on 10 June 1967, the Heights were in the hands of the IDF. At 7.30pm that night, Syria accepted the United Nations sponsored cease-fire and the war ended on the evening of the Sixth Day.

For the Israeli Air Force, it had been a long and hard campaign. They had flown 3,250 sorties over the six days, losing forty-six aircraft, (forty-three to ground fire and three in aerial combat). The first wave of attacks on the eleven Egyptian airfields involved one hundred and sixty Israeli aircraft, with one hundred and sixty-four being involved in the second wave which hit fourteen Egyptian airfields. At the end of the six days, the IAF had destroyed four hundred and fifty-two Arab aircraft, fifty-eight of these being shot down in air-to-air combat. Mirage IIICJs accounted for forty-eight aerial victories, fifteen of which were MiG-21s. Super-Mystère B2s scored five, Mystère IVs scored three, and one each to an Ouragan which shot down a MiG-17 and the Vautour II which shot down a Hawker Hunter.

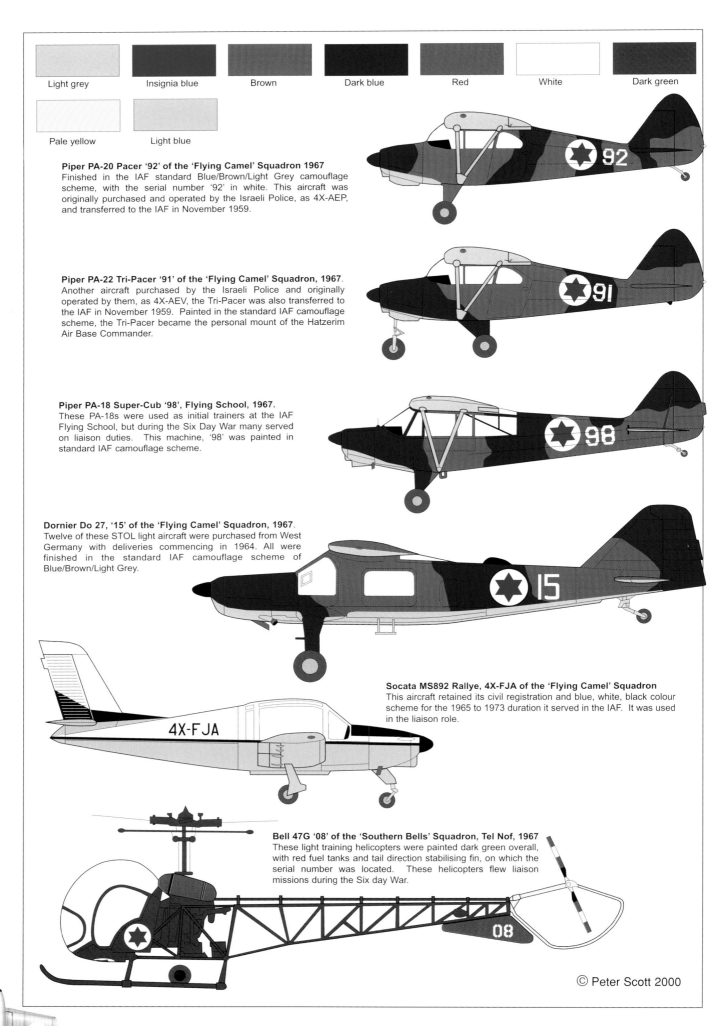

Light grey   Insignia blue   Brown   Dark blue   Red   White   Dark green

Pale yellow   Light blue

Piper PA-20 Pacer '92' of the 'Flying Camel' Squadron 1967
Finished in the IAF standard Blue/Brown/Light Grey camouflage scheme, with the serial number '92' in white. This aircraft was originally purchased and operated by the Israeli Police, as 4X-AEP, and transferred to the IAF in November 1959.

Piper PA-22 Tri-Pacer '91' of the 'Flying Camel' Squadron, 1967.
Another aircraft purchased by the Israeli Police and originally operated by them, as 4X-AEV, the Tri-Pacer was also transferred to the IAF in November 1959. Painted in the standard IAF camouflage scheme, the Tri-Pacer became the personal mount of the Hatzerim Air Base Commander.

Piper PA-18 Super-Cub '98', Flying School, 1967.
These PA-18s were used as initial trainers at the IAF Flying School, but during the Six Day War many served on liaison duties. This machine, '98' was painted in standard IAF camouflage scheme.

Dornier Do 27, '15' of the 'Flying Camel' Squadron, 1967.
Twelve of these STOL light aircraft were purchased from West Germany with deliveries commencing in 1964. All were finished in the standard IAF camouflage scheme of Blue/Brown/Light Grey.

Socata MS892 Rallye, 4X-FJA of the 'Flying Camel' Squadron
This aircraft retained its civil registration and blue, white, black colour scheme for the 1965 to 1973 duration it served in the IAF. It was used in the liaison role.

Bell 47G '08' of the 'Southern Bells' Squadron, Tel Nof, 1967
These light training helicopters were painted dark green overall, with red fuel tanks and tail direction stabilising fin, on which the serial number was located. These helicopters flew liaison missions during the Six day War.

© Peter Scott 2000

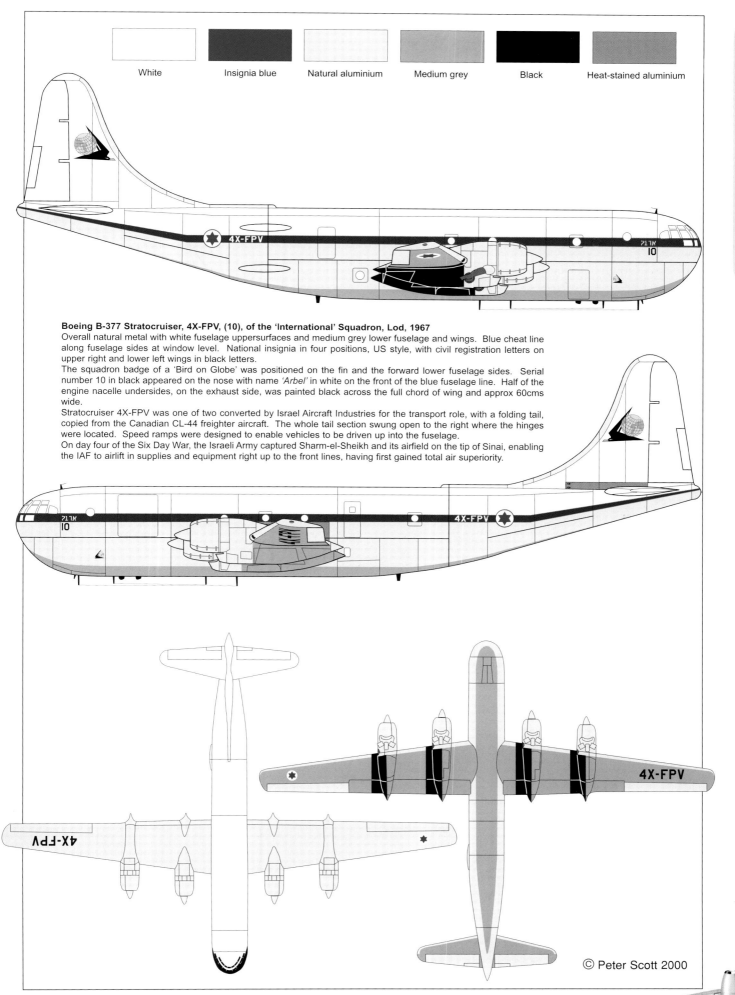

Colour swatches:

White   Insignia blue   Natural aluminium   Medium grey   Black   Heat-stained aluminium

4X-FPV אורבל 10

Boeing B-377 Stratocruiser, 4X-FPV, (10), of the 'International' Squadron, Lod, 1967

Overall natural metal with white fuselage uppersurfaces and medium grey lower fuselage and wings. Blue cheat line along fuselage sides at window level. National insignia in four positions, US style, with civil registration letters on upper right and lower left wings in black letters.

The squadron badge of a 'Bird on Globe' was positioned on the fin and the forward lower fuselage sides. Serial number 10 in black appeared on the nose with name 'Arbel' in white on the front of the blue fuselage line. Half of the engine nacelle undersides, on the exhaust side, was painted black across the full chord of wing and approx 60cms wide.

Stratocruiser 4X-FPV was one of two converted by Israel Aircraft Industries for the transport role, with a folding tail, copied from the Canadian CL-44 freighter aircraft. The whole tail section swung open to the right where the hinges were located. Speed ramps were designed to enable vehicles to be driven up into the fuselage.

On day four of the Six Day War, the Israeli Army captured Sharm-el-Sheikh and its airfield on the tip of Sinai, enabling the IAF to airlift in supplies and equipment right up to the front lines, having first gained total air superiority.

4X-FPV

10 אורבל

4X-FPV

4X-FPV

© Peter Scott 2000

Above: One of the 'clean' Flying School Fouga Magisters, coded '15', without the machine gun and rocket fit, in the 'operational' IAF Blue/Brown/Light Grey scheme, but with the yellow nose, tip tanks and fins. Note the small frontal area of the Magister which made them a difficult target to line-up on during head-on, close-support, ground attacks.

Above: Also participating in airlifting supplies to the Army at Sharm El Sheikh were the Boeing B-377 Stratocruisers, converted as transport aircraft for the IAF. Operated by the 'International' Squadron, 4X-FPV was one of two Boeing Stratocruisers to be modified with a 'swing-open' tail, like the Canadair CL-44 Transports.

Above: One of the mainstays of the IAF Transport Fleet was the Douglas Dakota. This particular example, 4X-FAK, painted in the standard IAF Blue/Brown/Light Grey scheme, was also equipped for Navigation Training, as illustrated by the DF fairings on the fuselage spine.

THE OPPOSING FORCES - JUNE 1967

ISRAEL

Operational Aircraft	
Mirage III	65
Super Mystere	35
Vautour	19
Mystere 4	33
Ouragan	51
Magisters	45
Total	**248**

Transports	
Nord Noratlas	23
Dakota	16
Stratocruiser	7
Total	**46**

Helicopters	
Super Frelon	4
Sikorsky S-58	25
Bell 47/Alouette II	13
Total	**45**

GRAND TOTALS	339

NEIGHBOURING ARAB STATES

Operational Aircraft	EGYPT	SYRIA	JORDAN	IRAQ	LEBANON	TOTALS
Tupolev Tu-16	30			10		40
Ilyushin Il-28	27	2		11		40
Mig 21	102	60		32		194
Mig 19	28					28
Sukhoi Su-7	16					16
Mig 15/17	96	35		30		161
Hunter			24	48	13	85
Vampire					18	18
Jet Provost				20		20
Total	**299**	**97**	**24**	**151**	**31**	**602**

Transports	EGYPT	SYRIA	JORDAN	IRAQ	LEBANON	TOTALS
Antonov An-12	25			8		33
Dakota			7	15		22
Ilyushin Il-14	58	5				63
Total	**83**	**5**	**7**	**23**		**118**

Helicopters	EGYPT	SYRIA	JORDAN	IRAQ	LEBANON	TOTALS
Mil 6	12					12
Mil 4	25	10		30		65
Wessex				20		20
Alouette III			4		5	9
Total	**37**	**10**	**4**	**50**	**5**	**106**

GRAND TOTALS	419	112	35	224	36	826

Chapter 6

Israeli Air Force Colours and Markings 1948 - 1967

Colours and Camouflage
Early Days

On the day of Independence in 1948, the *Sherut Avir* (Air Service) had acquired a number of aircraft all still in civilian guise and colours. This collection was to swell over the days and weeks ahead as different aircraft from all over the world were acquired and pressed into service.

Aviron light aircraft were mostly in a pale yellow colour or painted in silver dope as many had fabric covering. Following the attack on Sde Dov airfield on 15 May 1948, the order was issued to camouflage all the aircraft. However, this order did not state what the camouflage colours were to be nor did it specify any camouflage patterns for individual aircraft types.

Llight aircraft were located in to four Squadrons. Numbers 1 and 4 Squadrons were based at Sde Dov near Tel Aviv, with Number 2 Sqn (Negev) in the south at Nir-Am and Number 3 Sqn (Galil) based in the north at Yavneil in Galilee. Each Squadron obtained what paint they could and began to apply it to their aircraft, usually by brush.

The embryo Israeli Air Force had taken over many former RAF airfields, such as Ramat David, Kastina Aqir, Ein Shemer and Petah Tiqva. These airfields still held stocks of paint left by the former occupiers, and this was put to good use. Most aircraft were painted in RAF Dark

Earth and RAF Dark Green uppersurfaces, with either light grey (RAF Medium Sea Grey?) or the silver dope being retained on the undersurfaces.

Attempts were made to try and paint similar aircraft in roughly the same pattern, but as all three sites were being used, variations invariably did occur. In some cases RAF paint may have run out, or was not always available if operations prevented delivery. As a consequence some local improvisation on colours occurred particularly on Galilee-based aircraft where agricultural paint was available and used instead! Some of their aircraft were in darker shades of brown and green, but this was also more in keeping with the natural darker colours in that area.

Transport aircraft, such as the Lockheed Constellation, Douglas C-54 Skymaster, Douglas DC-3 Dakota and Curtiss C-46 Commando, retained their normal natural metal finish and markings as they were used predominently for trips overseas, on the supply runs to Israel. As the war progressed and the need for larger transports to be deployed on supply missions within Israel became apparent, and the aircraft allocated to that role were painted in camouflage colours.

Again there was no standardisation, with Dakotas being painted in green and brown colours and C-46 Commandos in

either brown or olive green uppersurfaces. There are photographs showing the roughness of the paintwork which was probably applied with a sweeping-brush. The undersurfaces were either painted in shades of light grey or just left in natural metal.

A good example of this non-standardisation are the three Boeing B-17G Flying Fortresses. No two aircraft were alike, with one aircraft, 1602, receiving a full upper surface camouflage of Dark Green, Light Green, Brown and Sand colours in a disruptive pattern. Another, 1601, operated in a grubby and dirty natural metal state, with the flaking paintwork markings of its previous owners. The aircraft were bought as 'scrap' and the need for operational missions was more important than their appearance.

As the IAF began to acquire fighter aircraft from abroad, standardisation did occur at least on some aircraft types. The Avia S-199s purchased from Czechoslovakia were painted overall in the greyish-green RLM 68 colour. This matched a standard Chech Air Force colour used prior to World War Two.

The Spitfires purchased from Czechoslovakia retained their standard RAF camouflage colours of Ocean Grey and Dark Green uppersurfaces and Medium Sea Grey undersurfaces. Following the clash with the RAF in January 1949, the upper surface camouflage colours were changed by replacing the Ocean Grey areas with a

Heading: Preserved Dassault 450 Ouragan at the IAF Museum at Hatzerim in authentic 'Hornet' Sqn markings, as it would have looked at the the time of the Suez Campaign in October 1956. Note 'sharkmouth', style of numerals and yellow and black recognition stripes.

Left: Another authentically preserved example at Hatzerim, this time showing a Spitfire Mk IXe in the original Dark Green/Ocean Grey/Medium Sea Grey scheme, as delivered from Czechoslovakia. White '26', 2011, served with 101 Sqn., and sports the unit's red/white rudder and spinner markings.

brown colour which was probably Dark Earth, differentiating these Spitfires from those used by the RAF. The brown was also more suitable for operations in that region.

Following the War of Independence, the IAF sought to establish itself as a modern airforce with modern command structures and facilites. The P-51D Mustang became its front line fighter, with the Spitfires gradually moving over to operational training role, and both aircraft types were operated in natural meta finishesl. The Mosquitoes acquired from France were painted silver overall, with the exception of the black-painted night fighter NF.30s and the few Trainer Yellow T.IIIs.

Silver dope was also the colour applied to training aircraft, as the Boeing Stearman Kaydets, Ansons and Consuls all appeared in this colour, generally also sporting red training bands around their wings and fuselage. However, the Harvards retained their camouflage colours of green and brown.

Standardisation

In early 1955, the IAF began to standardise on a new camouflage scheme following a new policy. Leading front-line aircraft, particularly those operating in the Day Air Defence of Israel would retain their natural metal finishes. All other operational aircraft types, and those which would assume an operational role in war-time, would be painted in a new scheme of Blue and Brown uppersurfaces and Light Grey undersurfaces. These colours were based on Israeli Paint Standards for which there are no direct BS 381 or FS 595 equivalents. However, RAL 5008 Blue, FS 30215 Brown and RAL 7044 Grey come close.

Up until 1969, the lead fighter aircraft in the IAF following the P-51D Mustang were the Gloster Meteor F.8, Dassault Ouragan, Dassault Mystsère IVA,

Below: Preserved Gloster Meteor F.8 at the IAF Museum - in the Blue/Brown/Light Grey scheme in use from early 1955 until mid 1967. Note the black/white markings on the nose tip and leading edges of the engine intakes which was common to all IAF flown Meteors, whether painted Aluminium or camouflaged.

Serial numbering system as at May 1948	
NB: In Hebrew, the letter/number was applied and read from right to left, but here below the serials have been printed from left to right for ease of reading	
Light Aircraft - A	
Austers	A-1 to A-20 (A-1, A-7 and A-13 = AOP.3s)
Tailorcraft	A-31 (VQ-PAI)
Auster Autocrat	A-32 (VQ-PAS)
RWD13	A-33 (VQ-PAM), A-34 (VQ-PAL)
Tailorcraft	A-34 (VQ-PAJ)
Piper Cub	A-50 to A-69
Medium and light transports - B	
Fairchild Argus	B-30 (VQ-PAM/1) to B-34
Beechcraft Bonanza	B-41 to B-43
Nord Norecrin	B-45 to B-46
Noorduyn Norseman	B-51 to B-56
Republic Seabee	B-61 (VQ-PAV)
Vultee BT-13 Valiant	B-62
North American Harvard	B-63 to B-68
Miles Aerovan	B-71
Grumman Widgeon	B-72 to B-73
Combat Aircraft	
Combat Aircraft (Fighters) - D	
Avia S-199	D-101 to D-124
Supermarine Spitfire Mk IX	D-130 to D-134
DH Mosquito PR.16	D-160
Bristol Beaufighter TF.X	D-170 to D-173
North American P-51D Mustang	D-190 to D-191
Bombers - H	
Boeing B-17G Fortress	H-1 to H-3
Large Transports - S	
DH Dragon Rapide	S-71 (VQ-PAR) to S-77
Douglas C-47 Dakota	S-81 to S-86

Dassault Super Mystère B2 and Dassault Mirage IIIC. As each aircraft entered service its predecessor was relegated to supporting roles and received the standard Blue/Brown camouflage Scheme. In 1969, with the entry of the F-4 Phantom and the adoption of a new camouflage scheme, the practice of retaining the lead aircraft in natural metal was abandoned.

Light training aircraft also changed colours during this period to overall Trainer Yellow applied to the Stearmans, Fokker S11s and some Harvards. Other Harvards had a weapons carrying capability and received the Blue/Brown camouflage with Yellow fuselage and wing markings.

The introduction of the Fouga Magister changed this as they all soon appeared in the Blue/Brown camouflage scheme with Yellow fuselage and wing markings. Later the Yellow areas were removed and the aircraft camouflaged overall. However, to emphasise its training role, strips of red flourescent tape were placed around the nose, tail-planes and wing-tip tanks. Several of the Fouga Magisters were re-equipped for ground-attack, and during the Six Day War in 1967, the red strips were simply removed to prepare it for its offensive role.

The standard Blue/Brown camouflage scheme was also applied to transport aircraft. However, some, like the Nord Noratlas, 4X-FAG, were retained in natural

metal as it was recognised that some overseas countries may be sensitive about a visit from an obviously looking warplane. Other transport-type aircraft, such as the Boeing B-377 Stratocruiser, were retained in their delivery colours as these would operate in roles or in areas where they would not need the application of tactical camouflage.

Two other exceptions to the standard camouflage rule were the Sikorsky S-58s received from West Germany which were painted in RAL 6014 Olive Green with the standard Israeli Brown applied to form a disruptive scheme. The Sud Aviation Super Frelons were painted in France with an uppersurface camouflage scheme of *Armée de l'Air* green and brown. Again a direct match is difficult, but the colours were close to FS 33448 Light Brown and FS 34102 Dark Green.

The standard Israeli Blue/Brown camouflage scheme was replaced during 1967, and had all but disappeared by the start of the 1970s.

National Insignia

With the creation of the State of Israel a national insignia was needed for the clear identification of its aircraft. The Shield of David, (in Hebrew = *Magen David*), was adopted for aircraft and after some experimentation, the blue six-pointed star on a circular white background was accepted.

As most of the aircraft at that time were light types such as Austers, an instruction was sent out for the painting of the new national insignia on these aircraft at the same time as they were being camouflaged. The instruction specified an 85cm diameter insignia on the upper and lower wings and a 45cm diameter *Magen David* on the fuselage sides.

Whilst this was initially adhered to, local improvisation became the norm as more types entered service and they needed to be ready for operations with minimum delay. There were also several shades of white and blue depending on what was available, and the size and shape of the *Magen David* could also vary, even on the same aircraft. At this time it was all hand painted.

With other aircraft types entering the IAF inventory, it was soon realised that the national insignia sizes issued for light aircraft did not have universal application, and discretion was given for the size of the *Magen David* to be appropriate to the aircraft type, with the proviso that it should be large enough to allow reasonable recognition.

When aircraft were acquired from overseas, the practice became that the *Magen Davids* applied were the same size and/or diameter as the original national markings/roundels they replaced. Thus *Magen Davids* appeared in diameter sizes of 45cm (18"), 62cm (24"), 85cm (33"), 91cm (36"), 100cm (39"), 107cm (42"), 115cm (45") and 122cm (48"). Eventually the IAF were to standardise on a style of national insignia and the colours of FS 17925 White and FS 35090 Insignia Blue.

Styles of Magen David
1 - Early Applications

This is typical of what could be found applied to early aircraft. The insignia was hand painted and often applied in haste, using colours available at the time.

2 - Standard Insignia

In the early 1950s, the IAF standardised on the style and colour of the *Magen David*. This was White FS 17925 and Insignia Blue FS 35090. Instructions were also issued as to the size of insignia for each aircraft type and their location on those aircraft.

3 - Standard Insignia with Insignia Blue outline

Concern that the white background could not be determined on aircraft painted white or silver led to the introduction of an Insignia Blue FS 35090 outline around the circumference of the white background.

4 - Smaller Star Variations

On aircraft purchased from abroad, particularly the DH Mosquitoes from France, the *Magen David* national insignia were applied before they left for Israel and consequently there was much variation. Typical of the style shown on Mosquitoes was a smaller star, in a lighter shade of blue from the standard colour adopted in Israel. When the aircraft went through maintenance, the *Magen David* was invariably replaced by the Standard Insignia version.

Campaign Markings
1 - War of Independence 1948

In the early part of the War of Independence, to aid recognition, identification bands were painted around the rear fuselage of many IAF aircraft. As these bands were usually applied at the same as the *Magen David*, the same colours were used. The bands would be White/Blue/White, however, there were no standard sizes or widths, so these varied aircraft to aircraft.

On larger aircraft such as Curtiss C-46 Commandos, these identification bands were also painted on the upper and lower surfaces of the wings. On seeing this, the Army told the IAF that they found identification easier from the wing markings and the next aircraft to arrive, the Spitfires from Czechoslovakia, only had White/Blue/White stripes applied to the undersides of the Wings.

By contrast the Bristol Beaufighters had two Blue stripes on a White band around the fuselage and the wings.

2 Operation Kadesh 1956

During the Suez Campaign of 1956, the IAF along with French and British Air Arms, applied Black and Yellow recognition stripes on their participating aircraft, but there were some exceptions, mainly on the Meteors. The first shots of the Campaign were fired by IAF Meteor NF.13, number 52, which didn't carry any of these 'Suez markings'. Other Meteors, particularly F.8s and PR.9s still in natual metal, only had a Black stripe painted around the rear fuselage, plus several also had an additional black stripe across the chord of both wings between the aileron and the engine nacelle .

These Black and/or Yellow stripes were usually applied by brush at each airbase so variations did occur. Generally the striping took the effect of equal width Yellow/Black/Yellow/Black/Yellow bands, whilst on some aircraft , it looked more like a broad Yellow band with narrower Black stripes.

Shortly after the Campaign, the stripes were removed.

Serial Numbers
The Israeli Air Force Aircraft Numbering System to 1967

Until independence in May 1948, the aircraft used by the *Sherut Avir* (Air Service) retained their civil registrations. The British manadated Territory of Palestine was allocated the International Registration VQ-P (for Palestine) for its aircraft, and the first to be registered were two Short S16 Scions, VQ-PAA and VQ-PAB of Palestine Airways in 1934.

When *Sherut Avir* was established it had the following aircraft on its books:-

Taylorcraft BL	VQ-PAI
Taylorcraft BL	VQ-PAJ
RWD 13	VQ-PAL
RWD 13	VQ-PAM
DH-82C (Canada) Tiger Moth	VQ-PAT
DH-82C (Canada) Tiger Moth	VQ-PAU
Auster J1 Autocrat	VQ-PAS
Dragon Rapide	VQ-PAR

At the end of 1947, Aviron Ltd purchased seventeen ex-RAF Auster AOP.5s and Auster AOP.3s for use by the *Sherut Avir*. Had the true 'end-user' been known the sale would probably not have been made, so these aircraft could not be given formal civilian registrations. *Sherut Avir* allocated each aircraft a number from 1 to 20, and as they were made airworthy again, they were painted in the same colours and given the registration of a 'legitimate' aircraft. For identification, each aircraft also retained its *Sherut Avir* number, which however was not actually painted on with the registration on the aircraft!

The 'legitimate' aircraft were:-
Tailorcraft VQ-PAI
Tailorcraft VQ-PAJ
Auster Autocrart VQ-PAS
Additional Auster allocations were:-
VQ-PAI/(2)
VQ-PAI/(4)
VQ-PAI/(5)
VQ-PAI/(6)
VQ-PAI/(9)
VQ-PAI/(10)
VQ-PAI/(11)
VQ-PAI/(12)
VQ-PAI/(14)
VQ-PAJ/(3)
VQ-PAJ/(8)
VQ-PAS/(1) (Auster AOP.3)
VQ-PAS/(7) (Auster AOP.3)

A Fairchild Argus, acquired at the same time, was allocated the registration of an RWD 13 to become VQ-PAM/(1). After this, the State of Israel was formed and the *Sherut Avir* became the Israeli Air Force with a new system of aircraft serial numbering.

Serial Numbering systems
- as at May 1948

The first numbering system involved grouping the aircraft into five different categories according to their role type and then allocating a number to each aircraft within those role types. Thus the aircraft serial number would be the role type identified by a Hebrew alphabet

Above: One of the various stencil styles of numerals applied to IAF aircraft - in this case on the preserved Ouragan at Hatzerim.
Below: Another stencil-style - this time on a preserved Vautour IIB.

character, (such as *Aleph*, *Bet* etc), followed by the individual aircraft number in arabic numerals, reading from right to left. The five role types were:-
• Light Aircraft = A
• Medium and Light Transports = B
• Combat Aircraft = D
• Bombers (eg B-17Gs) = H
• Larger Transports = S
This gave an inventory which looked like the list in the accompanying table above right.

- as at November 1948

In November 1948, the IAF introduced a new system of numbering which classified aircraft to their role, type, and an individual identification number based on the number of aircraft there were, starting with 01. Each aircraft was allocated a five digit number, but usually only the last four digits would appear on the aircraft, and eventually only the individual aircraft identity number was used.

Role Codes

Seaplane	1
Fighter	2
Fighter-Bomber	3
Medium Bomber	4
Heavy Bomber	5
Cargo Bomber	6
Transport	7
Liaison	8
Trainer	9

Aircraft Type Codes

Auster	01
Tailorcraft	02
RWD 13	03
Piper Cub	04
Argus	05
Bonanza	06
Norecrin	07
Norseman	08
Seabee	09
BT-13 Valiant	10
Harvard	11
Widgeon	12
DH Rapide	13
Dakota	14
DC-5	15
B-17 Fortress	16
Commando	17
DC-4	18
Avia S199	19
Spitfire	20

Israeli Air Force Serial Styles

1234567890
'Hebrew' style as worn by Stearmans, Ansons, Consuls etc.

1 1234567890
Thin brush stroke lettering as applied to Austers, medium brush stroke applied to others i.e. Avias (Note both types of 1).

X 1 T П Ɑ
Hebrew A   Hebrew B   Hebrew D   Hebrew H   Hebrew S

1 1234567890
Squat style as used on Harvards etc.

1234567890
Stencilled style as used on Mustangs.

1234567890
Stencilled style as used on Mustangs and Spitfires.

0123456789 9
Style as used on Fouga Magisters.

Mosquito	21
Beaufighter	22
Mustang	23
Constellation	24
Lodestar	25
Hudson	26
Stearman	27
Consul	28
Anson	29
Chipmunk	30
Fokker S11	31
Buckaroo	32
Hiller 360	33
Catalina	34

Thus, the serial for a Boeing B-17G Flying Fortress for instance would be: the number 5 for the role, ie Heavy Bomber; then 16 for the aircraft type, ie B-17G Fortress, then the individual aircraft number - in this case either 01, 02 or 03, as there were three B-17s in service. So the full serial numbers would be 51601, 51602 or 51603. However, only the last four digits usually ever appeared on the aircraft, eg 1601. Eventually, the role type figure was abandoned and the practice became to use only the individual aircraft number, which explains why the Hudson and the Lodestar for instance both carried the numeral 01.

The sytem used up to 1967
(and to some extent still in use today)
The arrival of new aircraft in the mid-1950s led the IAF to continue to allocate a two digit individual aircraft serial number as the permanent number of that aircraft. Thus the first Gloster Meteor F.8s were given numbers 01 to 11. However, the aircraft numbers were not always in straight sequences as the Meteor NF.13s were given numbers 50, 52, 55, 57 and 59.

In the 1960s, the practice continued when the seventy Dassault Mirage IIICs were numbered 01 to 80, so there were gaps and this was not a straight sequential run. The gaps cannot be accounted for except to say that there was no Mirage number 13, and 13 has not been allocated as a specific aircraft number on any aircraft type since this period. The IAF may be superstitious like other Air Forces. (eg the Fleet Air Arm used to fly Sea Harrier 12 and a half!). Later a prefix was added to the individual aircraft number and this seems to signify a particular upgrade, modification or role. Thus Mirages have appeared with the following numbers, 144, 259, 498 (Reconnaissance) 507, 753 and 942.

Above right: A preserved Mystère IVA with the 'Valley' Sqn badge on the fin.

Below: The 'Bat' Sqn badge under the cockpit of a preserved Meteor NF.13.

AIRCRAFT OF THE ISRAELI AIR FORCE IN SERVICE 1948 - 1967

DH Tiger Moth	1947 - 1948
Taylorcraft	1947 - 1949
RWD 13	1947 - 1950
Auster J/1, AOP.3, AOP.5	1947 - 1952
Lockheed Constellation	1948
Lockheed Lodestar	1948
Miles Aerovan	1948
Miles Gemini	1948
Avia S-199	1948 - 1949
Bristol Beaufighter TF.X	1948 - 1949
Douglas C-54 Skymaster	1948 - 1949
Douglas DC-5	1948 - 1949
Fairchild Argus	1948 - 1949
Grumman Widgeon	1948 - 1949
Nord Norecrin	1948 - 1949
Republic Seabee	1948 - 1949
Vultee BT-13 Valiant	1948 - 1949
DH Dragon Rapide	1948 - 1950
Curtiss C-46 Commando	1948 - 1952
Beechcraft Bonanza	1948 - 1953
Lockheed Hudson	1948 - 1954
Noorduyn Norseman	1948 - 1954
Avro Anson	1948 - 1956
Boeing B-17G Flying Fortress	1948 - 1956
Supermarine Spitfire Mk IX	1948 - 1956
DH Mosquito FB.VI, T.III, NF.30, PR.16, TR.33	1948 - 1957
Boeing Stearman PT-17 Kaydet	1948 - 1961
North American P-51D Mustang	1948 - 1961
North American Harvard	1948 - 1963
Douglas C-47 Dakota	1948 - Date
Piper PA-11 and PA-18 Super Cub	1948 - Date
DH Chipmunk	1949 - 1954
Temco T-35 Buckaroo	1949 - 1954
Airspeed Consul	1949 - 1956
Fokker S-11 Instructor	1949 - 1956
Consolidated Catalina	1951 - 1956
Hiller 360 and UH-12	1951 - 1959
Gloster Meteor F.8, T.7, FR. 9,NF.13	1953 - 1970
Dassault Ouragan	1955 - 1973
Nord 2501 Noratlas	1955 - 1978
Sikorsky S-55	1956 - 1963
Dassault Mystère IVA	1956 - 1971
Sud Aviation (Aerospatiale) Alouette II	1957 - 1975 & 1977-82
Sud Aviation Vautour II	1957 - 1971
Sikorsky S-58	1958 - 1969
Dassault Super Mystère B2 (& Sa'ar)	1958 - 1975
Piper PA-20 Pacer	1959 - 1969
Piper PA-22 Tri-Pacer	1959 - 1969
Beech 18	1960 - 1963
Fouga Magister/IAI Tzukit	1960 - Date
Dassault Mirage IIIC	1962 - 1982
Pilatus PC-6 Turbo Porter	1963 - 1968
Boeing 377 and KC-97 Stratocruiser	1964 - 1978
Dornier Do 27	1964 - 1982
Bell 47	1965 - 1968
Socata Rallye	1965 - 1973
Sud Aviation (Aerospatiale) Super Frelon	1966 - 1991